THE BRAIN-BASED BOSS

Adding serious value through employee engagement

THE BRAIN-BASED BOSS

Adding serious value through employee engagement

TERRY WILLIAMS

PUBLISHED BY:

seriouscomedy Limited

ISBN 978-0-47347-979-4

This product may be cited as: *The Brain-Based Boss*

Contents

About the Author

Terry's background is in corporate training and people management. He has a BA in History from Canterbury University and a Post grad Diploma in Business Administration majoring in Management from Massey University.

Author of *THE GUIDE: How to kiss, get a job and other stuff you need to know*, that book has been acclaimed as a platform for people to positively influence the young people in their lives.

As seen on TV1's *Good Morning* and TV3's *Sunrise*, Terry Williams combines humour with valuable business acumen to be a skilled and knowledgeable trainer, speaker or facilitator.

Terry consults to many New Zealand businesses in delivering frontline leadership training and strategic planning. His business card sometimes says Business Navigator which reflects his approach – trainees often already have the answers; what they're missing is the ability to move in the same direction, the right direction.

Before starting his companies seriouspeople Limited and seriouscomedy Limited, Terry worked in the financial services, gaming, telecommunications and local government sectors in training as well as operational and customer service management. Being a manager and business owner enabled him to have a greater involvement in broader organizational development but you'll see the spark of passion in him when he's in front of the room helping learners learn and, even more importantly, transferring that learning into practical, tangible and measurable results in the workplace.

Terry's point of difference as a speaker is that, in addition to his business experience and knowledge, he has also been a professional stand-up comedian for ten years. Often he's entertaining or hosting corporate events and conferences for clients such as Sony, Mercedes or the NZ Dairy Industry Awards. Consequently Terry's business presentations are engaging. Appropriate fun reinforces the learning.

Terry Williams trains, speaks and facilitates across the Asia-Pacific region and recently spoke to an HR Summit of 4500+ in Singapore. He is based in Auckland, New Zealand. He has two teenage children and challenges himself to do two dangerous things a year. (That's how he got into stand-up comedy.)

Acknowledgements

In the absence of that time machine that enables me to go back and give the young version of myself any advice, I thank Isabel Williams and Joshua Williams who, as leaders of the future, are an even better option.

Section 1

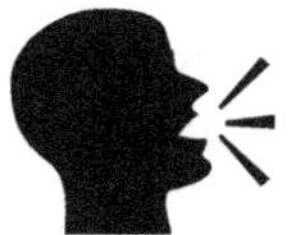

Why be a Brain-Based Boss?

The first section of this book presents the compelling reasons why you, as a leader in your workplace, should apply the Brain-Based way of doing things. Before I get carried away dazzling you with research findings and how you can apply them in your workplace, you're probably wondering if it's worth it. You should wonder. The research shows that the two fundamental questions in anyone's brain before they voluntarily attempt a new way of doing things are:

1. Is it worth it?
2. Can I do it?

I'll answer that first question with, 'Yes it is worth it'. Not because you think you should or because others say you should or because it's the latest trending management topic, but because the evidence proves that it increases productivity and profitability.

Research shows that 26% of employees are actively engaged and 28% actively disengaged. While the 28% is bad enough it is the remaining 46%, which are ambivalent, that you should be concerned about. Rather than over-investing time, money and energy to attract the rare and transient supertalented, I'm proposing that as a Brain-Based Boss, you'd be wiser to develop the 46%

you already have. How can we engage them to drive improved results?

The second section presents the research and introduces some questions for you on how you might apply each finding in your own workplace. The third section puts it all together, meshing my ideas on becoming a Brain-Based Boss with your own 'you-specific' ideas for you to try, tweak and try again.

And it has to be that way. No one can provide you with a prescriptive and universal approach to being an effective leader, even if a common question is, 'Why doesn't someone just tell me the one right way to lead people?'

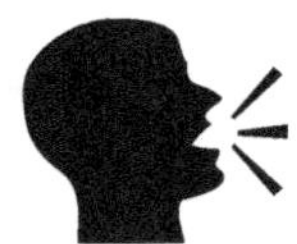

'One Right Way'?

When you first started leading people, did you expect your boss to take you aside and hand you a folder which had … *all the answers*? People have been leading people for centuries. The 'one right way' to lead people must have been written down, with updates continually being made and the latest version wet-inked, hot off the press, ready to be gifted to you now that you have earned the right to be responsible for the work of others.

In my early twenties, I got my first ever promotion to supervisor. I only had one person to supervise but that still counted. I waited for my folder full of answers. I didn't get it. I never did, after twenty five years. There is no 'one right way' written down. And there shouldn't be.

I accepted that there is no folder of answers early on and set about trying to learn, make mistakes and improve. My first thought was to find one person who was doing it successfully and model them, get them to teach me the ways of the 'force'. I was looking for the 'Obi Wan Kenobi' of leadership. I didn't find them. There is no 'Obi Wan Kenobi' of leadership. (Although, I have met quite a few Darth Vaders.)

Twenty five years later, I have my own bag of tools, rather than a written-down set of formal leadership procedures in a folder. I've gleaned these tools from lessons I've directly learned in supervisory and management roles, as well as observing the occasional 'Han Solo' of leadership along the way. I run leadership workshops and it's become something of a running gag that whenever I start a question with the phrase, 'What's the best way to …', there's a very good chance the answer is, 'It depends'. What's the best leadership style? What's the best way to motivate a worker whose well-earned nickname is 'Sleepy'? What's the best conflict management technique? It depends.

I'd love for there to be 'one right way' to lead people, to motivate Sleepy or to manage conflict. Plenty of people have written books with their 'one right way'. But there isn't. It really does depend. One of my good friends in the professional speaking business gave me a good old figurative slap across the face when I said semi-jokingly that my audiences were quoting my 'It depends' catchphrase. She said buyers of books and bookers of conferences weren't going to pay for, 'It depends'. They want to hear the latest 'one right way'. Surely, the fact that there is a 'latest' one right way implies that all the previous one right ways weren't, um, *right*?

This isn't a leadership metaphor, it's a comedy one, but the best way I've found to describe this way of thinking is the mental image of a CD. When you first start performing stand-up comedy, you go out on stage, you have five gags A, B, C, D and E and you deliver them A, B, C, D and E. Over time you'll develop more and more options until you're able to deliver the true illusion of spontaneous dialogue that is stand-up; a seemingly unique performance customised for the audience on that night. Your material is on a CD in your brain. You spin that disk. You walk out on stage and you give the remote control to the audience. It depends. This is equally true for Brain-Based Bosses in a workplace. The leader's approach should depend on the people involved, the context and the likely or desired consequences.

Quite apart from my own leadership experience, in researching this book alone I've also read over 100 books on psychology, plus I have a post-graduate diploma in business. The results of which is an even bigger bag of tools or CD spinning in my mind, but what's generally missing from the reading and the studying are specific and practical tools that frontline leaders can use on a day-to-day basis. They're interesting findings, provocative ideas, ground breaking research, and engaging tales but they're not tools.

For example, people with asymmetrical faces make better leaders. What?! I awoke one morning to the business news on the radio and that was the last 'human interest' item. Someone somewhere got research funding to assess the relative symmetry of people's faces and compared them to some subjective assessment of their success as leaders. (I'd like to see a study done on researchers who are successful at getting funding for spurious topics and see how asymmetrical their faces are once taxpayers find out.) I don't think, even if I'd been more awake, that their conclusion would have made any more sense. Apparently, good looking people don't have to try so hard and so end up with under-developed leadership and interpersonal skills. Asymmetrical people need to try harder and therefore do develop those skills. The asymmetrical poster child seems to be Winston Churchill. My problem with this and other similar research is – what possible application in the real world could these results have? Are the local hospitals supposed to employ an auditor in their maternity wards to measure the heads of newborns? 'Hmm, future head of state right there...'.

Are we supposed to add a new step to our recruitment processes to assess the symmetry of the applicant's face? Presumably we'll require recent photos to be included. If you're a high-flying ambitious type and you're a bit wonky in the visage department, there's always the option of reconstructive cosmetic surgery. No doubt there will be a smart phone app to do that for us. (There will possibly be people ready to believe that last bit anyway.)

Another piece of research showed that, in professional sports leagues, teams wearing black uniforms are penalised significantly more often than teams wearing other colours. Is this due to some latent racism or watching 'The Lone Ranger' too much as children? Who cares? (Other than fans of New Zealand rugby.)

The findings are *interesting* but, ***so what***?

So, what I've done with this book is take lots of interesting findings, provocative ideas, ground breaking research and engaging tales and apply to them the qualifying question, 'So, what?' Or, to give its full title: 'So, what does this do to help leaders improve results by influencing behaviour?' The result of which is a book of tools. It's not designed to be entry-level or comprehensive. I anticipate supervisors and team leaders in larger organisations and small business owners who have already tried the easy stuff that works *most of the time with most people* will find this book useful. I'm looking to help those of you having to deal with non-average situations. Maybe you've got a particularly challenging person, team or project? Maybe you're about to embark on a major change exercise and need to move a lot of people? Maybe you're experiencing unusual times and threats and need to attempt the big and different and it's only the challenge and threat that'll make it possible? Whatever your situation, this range of brain research turned into practical workplace techniques are a veritable smorgasbord of options. If every day is just another day at the office for you and you're happy with that, then maybe you'd be better off reading a cookbook or murder mystery? This book is for people trying to change behaviour to improve results.

Apart from interviews and articles, I've read over one hundred books researching for this one. I discovered a great number of interesting findings, just like the symmetrical faces study I mentioned earlier. However, being interesting wasn't enough for me for this book. The findings, studies, examples etc had to provide a workplace-relevant application for real leaders like you in the real world. It didn't pass that test for this book but I was amazed to read evidence that a monkey with a dart would pick better investments than most professional investment managers. And the more active in trading shares those investment managers were, the less successful they'd be over time. So, if you trusted the monkey to throw the darts, then the monkey retired and you had to stick with the original investment decisions, you'd be doing better than most people. Maybe that's already happening? Maybe that's how *Planet of the Apes* comes about rather than some genetically engineered airborne virus? The apes are already playing the stock market and the recession is part of the plan. See what I mean – interesting but not useful.

I also worried that maybe the research findings weren't universally applicable. Psych researchers have a hard enough job as it is so the easiest source of research subjects, historically, has been grad students. This has resulted in the over-sampling problem known as 'WEIRD' (Western, Educated, Industrialised, Rich and Democratic). There is a 4000% greater chance that a test subject has been a young American grad student rather than a random human being. Fear not. The guts of the important findings with regards to motivation have been tested and replicated in many non-WEIRD environments, including an especially impoverished part of India. The same conclusions were reached. My own publisher had concerns about whether to market this book in a particular country or internationally but once they saw the evidence they realised that when it comes to employee engagement, motivation and influence, people are people, be they normal or advantaged American grad students.

I've been leading people for over twenty years. I've read. I've studied. As a business trainer, I've delivered hundreds of programmes to thousands of people. Some of those programmes I have developed myself, others I've delivered on behalf of others. In researching this book, a recurring story about one particular piece of research that I'd used myself many times in training kept cropping up. It relates to a study at Yale where each member of the graduating class was asked if they had written down goals. 3% answered, 'Yes.' The results were noted and those people were tracked over the next twenty years. After those twenty years, it turned out that the combined net worth of the 3% who had written down goals was greater than the combined net worth of the other 97%.

Wow. I've used those findings, and seen them used by others, many times to validate the effectiveness of writing down properly developed goals. It's a powerful result. Well, it would be if that study ever took place, but it didn't.

You may have heard of that study. You might disbelieve me when I say it never took place. I still think writing down goals is a good idea; I'm not disrespecting that notion, but I challenge you to find any genuine citing of the original research.

I raise this point because I have ensured that every study described in this book cites the original researchers as best I can. If it's a clever idea that I think I thought of myself or if I can't remember the source, then I'll say so.

Non-existent research isn't the only problem I've discovered as I've tried to develop myself as a leader and change agent. Taking research out of context is another major problem.

When I'm delivering a presentation or running a training programme about communication or customer service, often I'll set the group a little exercise. I'll draw a pie chart on the board with three wedges, one 55%, one 38% and one 7%. Next to that I'll list three possible labels for the three wedges: **Body language**, **Voice**, **Words**. I'll frame the activity by saying something like, 'Research has shown that the first impression we make when we meet people is influenced by these three things but they each have different levels of influence. What wedges, do you think are the 55%, the 38% and the 7%? Pair up and debate with your buddy'. They get a couple of minutes; it generates a lot of noise and each pair reports back. The 'correct' answer is: **Body Language** 55%, **Voice** 38% and **Words** 7%.

This research did actually occur and the numbers it produced were as I wrote them above **BUT** I had taken it, as have so many other trainers and authors, *out of context.* The research was done within a very narrow context and was publicised into history before it could be validated or extrapolated beyond its narrow beginnings. You can't make such a gross over-simplification from a narrow experiment into broad areas such as 'communication' or 'customer service'.

In my defence, I always stress that to my readers and audiences. I ask them what the implications of this would be *if it were true.* I ask what the most important number is. Many say 55% but I say no. Eventually some bright spark twigs that the truly important number is *100%* - what matters is that you look like you mean what you say and you sound like you mean what you say. That's called congruence and it's very hard to find. Master that and you'll have a competitive advantage in most leadership roles. That's a legitimate use of the findings – to provoke the debate then set aside the individual numbers and focus on learning how to be congruent.

Besides, if you genuinely believe that 93% of the battle to communication is body language and tone of voice, then surely the next time you're in France trying to ask the price of a bottle of water from a retailer who insists they don't speak English, just shouting and waving your arms will get you through. (Tip: It won't **AND** the price of that bottle of water just went up.)

So, mythological research and out-of-context research are problems for us in our search to get better at learning how to influence behaviour change in others. In putting together all the findings in this book, I'm cautiously optimistic that I've avoided those two problems and one other. I'm not a psychologist myself, nor do I pretend to be one. (OK, I have pretended to be a psychologist more than once in my occasional role as conference entertainer with hilarious consequences.) I'm going to provide you with a quick once-over of a piece of research without going into dry and disinteresting detail. Then I'll provoke a few ideas on how this can be applied by you in the workplace. Then, I'll do it again and again until we run out of book. I may use a word like 'Heuristic' because a psychologist used it but, rest assured, I had to look it up. (It's a mental rule of thumb that provides our brains with rough and ready answers to problems, serving to indicate or point out; stimulating interest as a means of furthering investigation.)

The third problem with some research for me is the trust and credibility of the source. If I'm in a conversation or a non-critical portion of a presentation about to cite research and I can't recall a credible source, I'll always predicate my remarks with something like, 'Don't quote me on this,' 'I might have seen this on TV so who knows if it's true but ...', 'Just for the sake of the argument, let's assume that there is some research that shows that...' That approach is fine for a throwaway remark in an informal setting. It isn't for this book.

There is a critical piece of research that is probably the experiment most often cited in all the books I read in my research. I'll detail it later but, briefly, it was originally conducted by a fellow called Mischel and it involved offering children a treat now or two treats later if they could wait. This indicated their level of gratification-delaying ability and those with it turned out to be more successful in later life. BUT in some reading, the treats were marshmallows and in some the treats were Oreo cookies. Who am I supposed to believe? It's only a seemingly small detail but it matters. As it happens, I found out and I'll let you know later along with how we can develop that gratification-delaying ability in ourselves and others and how that can contribute to better results for us. Take a break from reading now because you're probably in the mood for a snack.

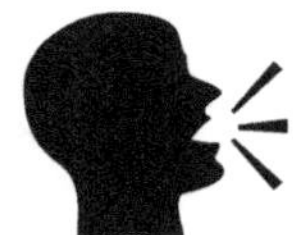

Brain 'Porn'

A few critics have slammed the rise of so-called 'Brain-Porn'. They slate the slew of self-help books coming out that cite studies which plug people into machines and show which bits of their brain glow under different stimuli and so forth. Supposedly, charlatans just add the prefix 'Neuro' to anything to sell books, webinars and tickets to workshops. Neuro-economics, Neuro-retailing, Neuro-tiddlywinks. I'm happy that my book's title contains the word 'Brain' and I do cite some research which involves brain scans. To me, it's more important that the research provokes ideas that might be useful in the workplace. The critics are right in that in business thinking (as in hairstyles) there are waves of new fads that get relegated to history by the next one.

Self Awareness First

'Know thyself.' – Inscribed at the
Temple Of Apollo, Delphi, Greece.

The Anablep is a type of fish found in Central and South America. It is also a metaphor I use in my training and writing. Its local nickname is 'the four-eyed fish'. It doesn't literally have four eyes but its two eyes each have two divisions that function, effectively, as separate eyes. It's primarily a surface dwelling floater and, as such, can be preyed upon from above by birds and from below by bigger fish (there's always a bigger fish). The Anablep can see above and below the waterline *at the same time*! I don't know if you believe in a God or Gods or mother-nature or pixies but that something like the Anablep can exist and evolve through random chance is, if not a miracle, incredibly cool.

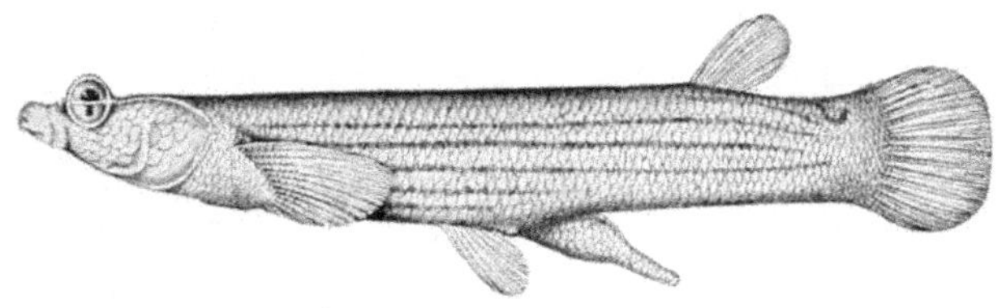

Coolness in reality aside, it's also a cool metaphor as it represents the need to look at a situation on two levels at the same time. One of the primary means of developing yourself is receiving feedback on your performance. It'd be great if you had a coach following and observing you and providing you with behaviour-based, esteem-building, specific and timely feedback at all hours. But you don't. No one does. But – wherever you go, there you are. To be able to observe yourself in action, as objectively as possible, and give yourself feedback is a major development accelerant. Just like the Anablep, you watch the person you're having a sales conversation or performance discussion with and, at the same time, observe yourself in action.

It's called 'Metacognition' – *thinking about thinking*. Our awareness of other people's states depends on how well we know our own. It's the starting point to get away from ingrained behaviours and habitual responses. It's the first step towards moving beyond reactive emotional loops. When it comes to emotional states, if you can name them you can tame them. 'I am sad' is very different to 'I feel sad' .

We can develop our own Metacognition skills with some very practical steps that actually result in changing the physical structure of our brain. Neurons that fire together, wire together. Later we'll learn about the mirror neuron system, thanks to an Italian research student in the mid-1990s who helped himself to some peanuts that were supposed to be for a watching monkey whose brain happened to be connected to a scanner. Not so much 'monkey-see, monkey-do' as 'monkey's brain see, monkey's brain mirrors'.

What I'd suggest would be most useful to you as you read this book is to try and see the information from two points of view, as the Anablep would. Firstly, what are the implications for yourself? Secondly, how might you apply each technique with the people you lead.

As you read through this book and reflect upon each of the ideas, consider how to apply them practically in your own situation. Read with a pencil in hand because there's space for you to make notes as you go. Focus particularly on three questions after each major topic:

1. What does this idea mean for you personally?
2. What might this idea have to do with someone you lead?
3. Thinking about that particular person you lead, how might you tweak your style in dealing with them to be more effective?

Throughout this book, I'll sprinkle in a few practical applications of Brain-Based Boss ideas that I've witnessed in action in real workplaces. I'll call them 'Brain-Based Seeds of An Idea'. Here's the first:

Brain-Based Boss Seed Of An Idea

I worked with a lawyer at a bank who, whenever she was taking notes in a meeting, used a two-columned notepad. One column was for notes about the task that most people would take in a meeting. In the other column she would write words and phrases used repeatedly by others at the meeting which she would make special effort to use back to them. Simple, free and incredibly impactful. A practical application of the Anablep metaphor – thinking about thinking with business results in mind.

You Can't Motivate Anyone!

Thomas Gilovich, a leading psychologist looking into decision-making and behavioural economics, said, 'One of the most important findings from my field of psychology is that the tiniest little change in circumstance can have big impacts on people's behaviour'.

Maybe you're one of those managers who say things like, 'They're paid to show up and do a job, they should show up and do that job'? OK, fair enough. Go with that. Technically, you're right. People *should.* All this psych, touchy-feely mumbo-jumbo is a waste of time.

It'd be a much simpler and duller world if that was true but it isn't. In 1982, neurologist Antonio Damagio showed with his patient 'Elliot' that our brains cannot make rational decisions without emotional processing. 'Elliot' had an accident which damaged the part of his brain that processed emotions. As a result, he suffered from pathological indecision. That has nothing to do with 'shoulds' or 'shouldn'ts' but is simply a fact of our physical and mental systems.

You'll read research later in this book about how to help people harness their subconscious and emotions to make better decisions and generate greater success at work. I always suspected that was true but I never suspected that without that emotional processing going on subconsciously, we wouldn't just make inferior decisions, *we'd be unable to make any decisions at all.*

In 1997, Antoine Bechara and Hanna Demasio conducted an experiment demonstrating the relative usefulness of our conscious and automatic systems and, more importantly, they are at their best when they are working together. Participants sat before a table on which were four stacks of cards. The participants had sensors attached to their fingertips measuring their skin conductive response – an indicator of heightened activity within the automatic nervous system. Unbeknownst to them, the stacks of cards were loaded. Two were predominantly full of 'bad' cards and two full of predominantly 'good' cards. They set about picking cards, winning or losing money as they went. The average number of cards taken before the participants consciously worked out which were the good decks was 25. The automatic nervous system had it sussed after 13 cards.

If you choose to take this research as justification to hit Vegas and 'go with your gut,' just remember, the house always wins.

And again, to those leaders who believe that their people should do as they told and follow instructions, here's a little bit of research about people. Let's assume that most people deeply care about their infant children. We are compelled, by law, to use child-restraints and car seats that comply with specified safety standards. A survey done of such car seats found that 73% were installed incorrectly to such a degree that it would fail to protect the child. These aren't uncaring parents who were surveyed. They went to the trouble of getting the car seats and installing them, but, on something of life-and-death importance to these people, they hadn't followed instructions. Sure, we can blame the writer of the instruction manual but doesn't this confirm your experiences of assembling kitset furniture at home or any number of situations at work? People are people so let's try as leaders to work with their natural and automatic response systems rather than try and fail to arbitrarily impose external and artificial control systems – their use is limited and inefficient.

Edward L Deci, the co-founder of self determination theory, says, 'The proper question is not, "How can people motivate others?" But rather, "How can people create the conditions within which others will motivate themselves?"'

People Are Our Greatest Asset

Your workplace or HR department might exclaim loudly that 'Our people are our greatest asset'. Do you know who the first person to make that statement was?

It was Joseph Stalin.

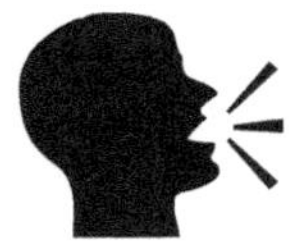

Employee Engagement

Whatever most leaders are doing right now isn't working!

Employee engagement is an employee's willingness to apply discretionary effort into their work. Researchers John Roberts Associates (JRA) define it as the extent to which employees are motivated to contribute to organisational success and are willing to apply discretionary effort to accomplishing tasks important to the achievement of organisational goals. Basically, engagement is choosing to do more than you have to. It isn't happiness or morale or anything people might say they think they think on a self survey. Its only measure is observable behaviour.

Wearing my comedy hat, one of my clients would run a V8 motor racing team and I would host their corporate hospitality. Part of that job would involve collecting up guests' business cards to go in the draw for a chance to win a hotlap with the famous driver Greg Murphy. One time I was assigned a team of 'promo girls' to collect up the business cards in their cowgirl hats. In ninety minutes, from a crowd of seven hundred guests, they managed to collect four cards. I'm sure some promo girls are funding their degrees in neuro-surgery but this particular crew was an example of disengaged employees. Probably, to be more accurate and fair, this would be an example of me failing to engage them.

Conversely, another day I was dragged into a shop on Waiheke Island. It was a soap and candle shop and, as I'm not really a soap and candle kind of guy, my attention was wandering. The exuberant shop assistant behind the counter was not only providing great customer service to a lady but was also telling her how excited she was about starting her new job here at the store. Only then did I notice the shop hours sign on the door. The store wasn't even supposed to be open. That's an engaged employee.

Employee Engagement is not a management-speak term for employee happiness or morale or anything like that. We've all heard the term 'absenteeism' for when employees don't show up for work (for whatever reason, legitimate or otherwise), but have you heard the term 'presentism' for when employees are physically present but they're not really there in spirit?

Does it make a difference if they're engaged or merely 'present'? Should you care if your people are 'engaged' in their work? Workforces with predominantly engaged employees are more profitable, retain staff better, attract a higher calibre of applicants and benefit from healthier people. A study in Singapore estimated that the cost of disengagement to their economy annually was 4.9 billion dollars.

Engaged employees are getting some meaning from their work and that's a fundamental human need. In today's busy world, if we don't get recognition, satisfaction and respect from our work, where are we going to get it from?

Much of the engagement research I'm about to summarise comes from studies conducted by research companies Towers Perrin and JRA over the past ten years.

One particular UK survey was typical of the proportions of average workplace engagement:

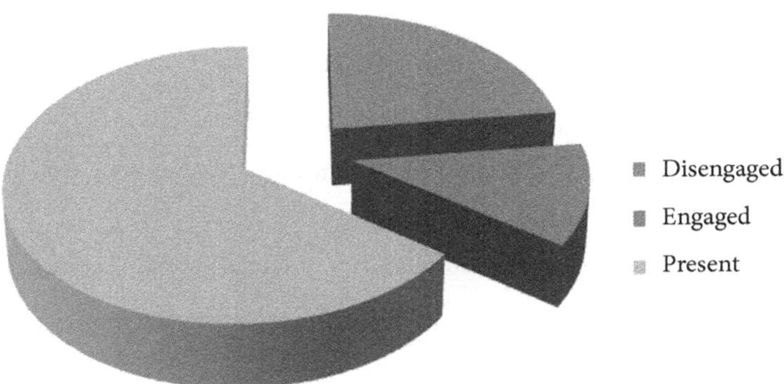

With averages, the devil is in the detail. The average engaged population was 12% but for management it was 20%, inflating the average. For non-management, it was 9%!

Without paying some consultants to rock on in and charge you for surveying your people, how can you tell if you have an engaged workplace?

- When you stop and ask random people how their work contributes to the success of the organisation, they can tell you specifically.
- They care about the future of the workplace.
- They would recommend to their friends that they work there.
- They tell people where they work without hesitation.
- They believe their performance has a direct impact on the

financial performance of the company (If you treat employees as if they make a difference to the company, they will).

What are clues of a disengaged workplace?

- Actively seeking employment elsewhere.
- Total focus on pay.
- Speaking poorly of the employer.
- Critical of managers and co-workers.
- Disproportionately spending time on personal activities during work time.
- Refusal to do any more than the specified minimum requirements.
- A spike in absenteeism.

Since 2010, Gallup has conducted a major quarterly study on employee engagement in the United States.

	Q4 2010	Q1 2011	Q2 2011	Q3 2011
% Engaged	28	30	30	29
% Unengaged	53	52	51	52
% Actively Disengaged	19	18	19	19

The percentages vary slightly across industries, countries and time but, broadly speaking, there's a minority at either end of the scale who are either really into their jobs or really not into their jobs, and a bulk of people in the middle who just show up. Gallup's been studying this in depth since 2000 and the highest ever engagement levels came in 2001, 2002, 2006 and 2007 when the record level was ... 30%. So, from a record high of 30%, the worst economic conditions internationally in our lifetime has caused engagement levels to plummet to ... 29%. What!? Perhaps money isn't a major influence here? More soon on that shocking news for our logical minds.

Gallup offers a few high-level observations. The better educated are significantly less engaged. (Perhaps ignorance really is bliss?) Middle-aged workers are less likely to be engaged.

Older workers are highly engaged. Males are much less likely to be engaged. Engaged employees perform on average 20% better. They are 87% less likely to leave.

The phrase 'Employee Engagement' might be a recent development in management jargon but the concept is timeless and easily recognisable to anyone who has ever worked. Corinne Maier even wrote a book in France called *Hello Laziness – Why Hard Work Doesn't Pay*. Her stats claimed 17% of French employees were actively disengaged and only 3% engaged.

Bosses who assist their people in identifying their personal values raise engagement levels, causing a 20% jump in discretionary effort and lowering the likelihood of that person leaving the organisation by 87%.

Disengagement won't happen overnight (but it will happen if you don't take control of the motivational environment). Disengagement is a process.

Recognise the symptoms along the continuum and you'll be in a far more powerful position to do something about it.

Factors that, looked at together, give an indication of employee engagement with a team are:

- Overall employee satisfaction.
- Likelihood of recommending a friend to work there.
- Likelihood of recommending the company's products and services to friends.
- Intention to stay at least two more years.
- Willingness to give extra effort, especially if not asked.

From a survey across sixteen countries, Towers Perrin identified the top ten drivers of employee engagement, in order, as:

1. Senior management is interested in employee wellbeing.
2. I have improved my skills over the past year.
3. We have a reputation as a good employer.
4. I have input in the decision-making in my department.
5. Pay/Benefits.
6. This organisation focuses on customer satisfaction.
7. My manager inspires enthusiasm.
8. The salary criteria here are fair and consistent.
9. There are opportunities here to learn further.
10. Employees here understand how to satisfy customers.

Other surveys have slightly different results and they do vary a bit across countries, time and industry but this is a good starting point.

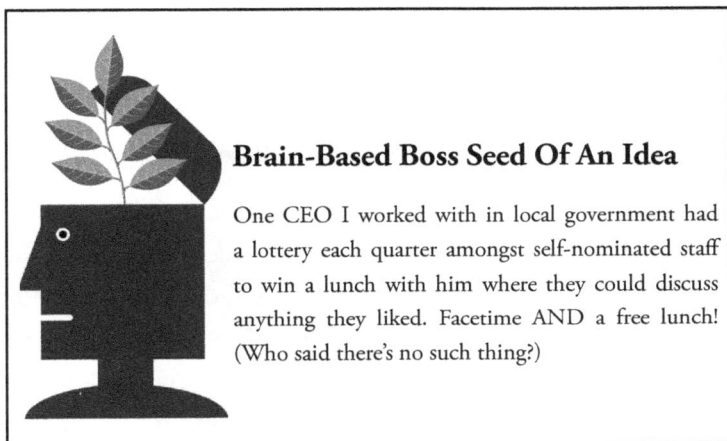

Brain-Based Boss Seed Of An Idea

One CEO I worked with in local government had a lottery each quarter amongst self-nominated staff to win a lunch with him where they could discuss anything they liked. Facetime AND a free lunch! (Who said there's no such thing?)

Is It Worth It?

The short answer is, 'Yes'. Being a Brain-Based Boss is worth it.

In my travels, I still come across a determined, but decreasing, number of managers and business owners who are of the view that employees are paid to do a job and they should bloody well show up and do it. 'We're not running a bloody day care centre here!' As Oscar Wilde said to an actor, 'Your motivation is in your pay packet'. Just because it sounds like it's a good idea and lots of people say you *should* have an engaged workplace, what's in it for you as leader? Here are just a few findings. Companies with above average employee engagement have:

- significantly higher operating margins relative to their industry. A 15% increase in engagement correlates to a 2.2% increase in operating margins;
- lower staff turnover and associated direct and indirect costs (a popular rule of thumb is that the direct cost of replacing an employee is their annual salary);
- lower absenteeism;
- higher customer satisfaction;
- better safety records;
- higher quality and more efficient production;
- less 'shrinkage' (theft by staff).

JRA found in New Zealand that a 10% increase in engagement led to a $NZ12,130 increase in earnings per employee and a 2.4% reduction in annual staff turnover. Remember that rule of thumb that the cost of replacing an employee is about their annual salary? Do the math.

Average Return On Assets

Engagement	Low	Medium	High
Return On Assets	6%	9.8%	22.8%

So, given all these glaring positive results for engaged workplaces, where do the challenges lie in creating more workplaces that are engaged? Roughly a tenth of employees are actively disengaged and two-thirds merely show up and do what they have to. Even if we write off the disenchanted, there's a lot of latent potential in that two thirds. It's easier, cheaper and quicker to work with this existing group than to try and attract, recruit and retain high-flying superstars who arrive already pre-motivated, although you should try and do that too when the opportunity arises.

You've read the lists of engagement drivers in their ranked order of effectiveness. Where do the challenges lie? Where should you start first in your engagement enhancement efforts? Bear in mind that all these stats are averages and your workplace may well be non-average, so your first steps should revolve around information gathering, observation and measurement to see where your particular strengths and opportunities lie.

That said, let's look at those averages. Of employees:

- 35% believe their manager understands what motivates them as individuals.

- 51% believe their manager encourages initiative.
- 28% believe their base pay is fair.
- 46% believe they will share in their organisation's successes.
- 34% believe their organisation provides them with challenging work.
- 23% believe advancement is based on performance.

Of managers:

- 96% want to be good communicators and listeners but only 43% believe they are (that's not to say they are good, just that they believe they are).
- 79% want their vision to be shared but only 38% believe that it is.

Lack of trust is a major obstacle to developing a culture of engagement. We cannot erase the past few decades of jobs being replaced by robots, outsourcing, globalism, corporate spin, grotesque fat-cat pay disparities between frontline and executives, changing rules retrospectively and having reward systems increasingly more aligned with the goals of senior management only. These things aren't all inherently bad, however. I, for one, think that any job a robot can do is probably best done by a robot.

For society, this was supposed to free up humans for leisure, family and more meaningful activities. A recent study done in South Korea and Japan looked at what workers did with their bonus hours during periods in their economic development where there was a significant increase in the average leisure time.

Some may have looked to cure cancer or create exquisite art in their spare time, but the two main areas of discretionary activity growth were TV watching and personal grooming.

A UK survey on trust by the Chartered Institute of Personnel and Development in 2005 showed 41% of employees had little or no trust in senior management and a 10% decline in trust in their immediate managers during the previous two years. Of those with less than a year's service, 57% trusted management communication. For those with more than fifteen years' service, the figure was 25%. Again, these are UK results and averages. What's important to you is what's real to you. Find out!

Chief Executives of large companies with Human Resource departments can go out and commission external consultants to conduct surveys and provide recommendations. When Government and the media talk about workplaces, large companies are often who gets talked about. However, the vast majority of employees work in workplaces with ten or fewer employees. They don't have a Human Resource department and aren't going to commission consultants. Nevertheless the same potential benefits are there for these workplaces if they can get their people predominantly engaged. The first steps are the same regardless of the scale or nature of the workplace. Find out, however informally and DIY, how you are doing today. Observe and ask around. Look at the information you do have for clues. How's the staff turnover? How's absenteeism? Do people park their cars at the start of the day in the way that'll enable them to make the quickest possible get-away at the end of the day, indicating that even before they start work their mindset is all about not being there? (I saw this latter point in a recent survey. I include it more for humour as it wasn't that scientific a survey but still it makes you wonder...)

Surveys are all well and good, and beliefs are important, because an employee's perception is effectively their reality, but just because only 28% believe their base pay is fair doesn't mean that the base pay is unfair. People used to believe that the Earth was flat and the universe revolved around it. I don't think surveys would've helped Galileo, Copernicus or Magellan.

If you are taking the DIY route, what should you look at? Start with employee satisfaction, advocacy and discretionary effort. After you're done gathering information, then you should start taking action. Why? JRA found that there was too much focus on the lowest rated drivers of engagement in efforts by managers to improve it. Just because the average number one driver of employee engagement in your country is x, doesn't mean that yours is x. You need to determine the relative importance of each driver in your workplace first.

VISION AND VALUES	
I have confidence in leadership	71%
Sense of common purpose	69%
I believe in what we're trying to accomplish	83%
SENSE OF COMMUNITY	
I feel a sense of belonging	73%
Fun	66%

LEARNING AND DEVELOPMENT	
I have a sense of personal achievement	77%
I make full use of my knowledge and skills	69%
I am encouraged to try new things	69%
PERFORMANCE CULTURE	
I feel my contribution is valued	66%
We celebrate success	71%

Remember the Towers Perrin top ten list of engagement drivers earlier? Here's a more useful list from JRA in New Zealand from 2010. Their top ten accounts for 77% of the influence over engagement but as you can see that average 77% varies across the drivers. Target those with a higher relative importance first.

A Saratoga Institute study in 2003 reinforced a commonly found gap between the perception of employers and employees. 89% of employers believe that those employees who leave do so for more money elsewhere. That belief is held by 12% of employees. Why then do they actually exit? Why do those who stay, stay? Perhaps a more useful question would be what can you do to encourage those you want to stay to stay?

What are the leaders in the highly engaged workplaces doing?

- During recruitment, they emphasise compatibility ('Fit') of values between the applicant and the workplace.(We talk much more later about this concept of 'Fit'.)
- They share knowledge between teams.

- They run frequent informal team mixer events.
- They monitor employee well-being, not just in surveys but with genuine personal enquiry.
- They support training.
- They have succession and talent plans.
- They make development of other leaders a high priority.
- They support coaching and mentoring.
- They try informal learning such as job rotation.
- They provide and insist on regular quality feedback and expect that of others.
- They demonstrate that they manage people's poor performance fairly but effectively.
- They recognise individual and collective achievements in a variety of ways.

And in doing those things above, what are they trying to achieve that goes towards stimulating everyone's sense of engagement?:

- Alignment of personal and team goals as much as practicable.
- Becoming active, if not necessarily perfect, communicators.
- Eliminating 'they' and 'them' when teammates are talking about each other.
- Self generated peer-to-peer recognition.
- A consistently understood and agreed sense of building something together.
- The elimination of defensiveness.

Interestingly, JRA found that employees tend to be more engaged during tough times and less so during good times. Why?

There's shared purpose – a joint fight for survival. Plus, there are more options for less-than-engaged employees in the good times to seek out the perceived greener grass elsewhere or at least take the risk in looking.

Leigh Branham, in his book *The 7 Hidden Reasons Employees Leave*, identifies what he sees as the main push factors for employees:

1. The workplace did not match expectations.
2. A mismatch between the person and the job.
3. Too little coaching and feedback.
4. Too few growth and advancement opportunities.
5. Feeling devalued and unrecognised.
6. Stress from overwork and a work-life imbalance.
7. Loss of trust and confidence in senior leadership.

The foundation for these push factors is a set of human needs that will become very familiar very soon. These aren't good old Maslow's hierarchy of needs. These are our mental needs:

- For trust.
- To have hope.
- To feel a sense of worth.
- To feel competent.

What are some of the tools currently used by many leaders in trying to motivate others? Threats, rewards, deadlines, imposed goals, surveillance, evaluations, competitions. Edward Deci argues that, just as the physical body has needs, so too does the mind. Three needs in particular he identifies are relatedness, autonomy and a sense of balance between competence and challenge. There is a very human need for 'behaviour – outcome linkages' or meaningful contingencies. Simply put, *we need to feel that what we do makes a difference.*

An inconsistent or chaotic environment produces amotivation – the absence of motivation which isn't quite demotivation but it isn't what we want. A controlling environment produces compliance or defiance. The true test of the workplace environment you've created is what happens when you're not around. As Deci says, 'The real job involves facilitating their doing the activities of their own volition, at their own initiative, so they will grow doing the activities freely in the future when we are no longer there'.

Brain-Based Boss Seed Of An Idea

I worked with a call centre that was planning a move and a re-fit which meant major disruption to, and extra effort from, the staff. Discretionary design and decor decisions were shortlisted by management and designers but then put to the staff for the final decision.

Section Two

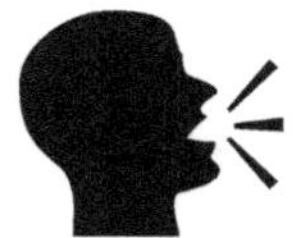

The 5 Principles Of Brain-Based Bosses

According to Daniel Pink, any leader of a workplace environment that initiates and supports self motivation needs to nurture people's sense of *autonomy*, *mastery* and *purpose*. My view is that the foundation, and the first step in any personal development, starts with *self awareness*. We need to be able to observe ourselves and provide ourselves feedback with our 'Anablep' eyes. Over time, you'll be leading teams of people at various stages along the self motivation road and some of them will be up to the deliberate *influence* of others. Based on this, I've subdivided all the brain research I'm including under five key principles:

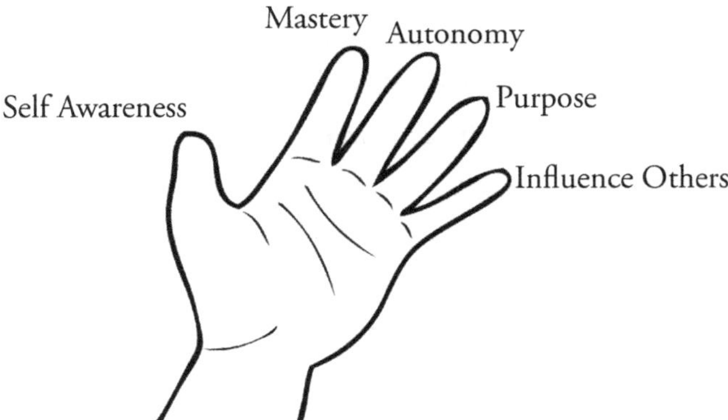

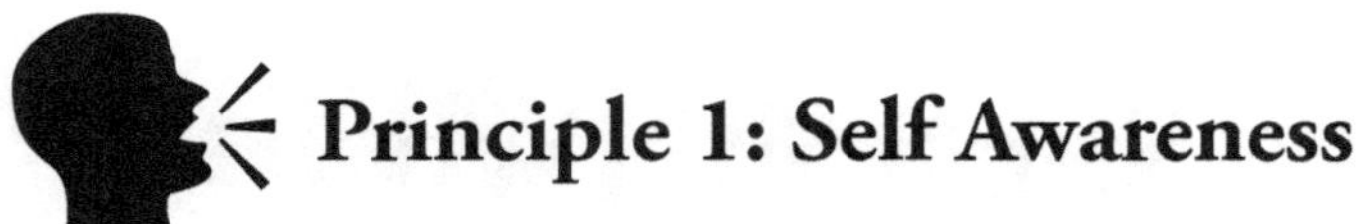

Principle 1: Self Awareness

Self Discipline (Don't Eat The Marshmallow)

In 1968, psychologist Walter Mischel, then at Stanford University, conducted a study on pre-schoolers at the Bing Nursery School on campus. (In fairness, his daughters attended there.) Each child was put in a small room with just a table and chair, and presented with a tray of potential treats. Options included marshmallows, Oreo cookies and pretzels. Marshmallows were the most popular. Each child was told that they could select one treat and have it immediately or, if they waited until the researcher returned in 'a few minutes', they could have a second treat. If they ate their first treat at any stage before the researcher returned, there would be no second treat.

This seemingly silly and fun study, much of which looked like scenes out of TV's *Candid Camera*, eventually showed that some behavioural traits are highly predictive. Jonah Lehrer interviewed some of these children for *The New Yorker*. He did so forty years after the experiments. Mischel had followed their progress as young adults since 1981. Lehrer quotes one former nursery school student Craig, 'I took everything I could,' he says. 'I cleaned them out. After that, I noticed the teachers encouraged me to not go into the experiment room anymore'.

They filmed the experiments. Look for them on YouTube,

especially the kid who furtively glances around, splits open an Oreo cookie, licks out the icing, puts the cookie back together again and returns the empty cookie to the tray. Classic!

Not everyone was like Craig. 30% resisted successfully for the entire time the researcher was away and earned their bonus. Did it make any difference in later life if you were a 'grabber' or a 'delayer'? Grabbers were more likely to have behavioural problems, both in school and at home. They got lower S.A.T. scores. They struggled in stressful situations, often had trouble paying attention, and found it difficult to maintain friendships. Craig, a grabber, lives in Los Angeles and does 'all sorts of things'. He's currently 'working on his first screenplay' – a euphemism for unsuccessful if ever I heard one.

On many measures of success, the deferring children went on to do better than the grabbing children in finances, academics, relationships, health, and happiness. Deferred gratification is an aspect of self discipline and impulse control which Daniel Goleman identified as a pillar of emotional intelligence. Maybe you started out thinking about whether your own kids are grabbers or deferrers but now you're thinking back to *your own* childhood ... How you doin'!?

Ozlum Ayduk, a psychologist from Berkeley, found that grabbers end up as adults with a higher than average body mass and more drug problems. They really can't 'just say no'. Mischel showed that the ability to delay gratification is a critical success factor in life. At the time of writing, researchers are beginning to scan the brains of grabbers and delayers to see what is going on inside their brains. That's of little use to us. You're a leader trying to help those you lead succeed. You probably don't have access to a brain scanner at work or even a photocopier that doesn't jam three times a day. However, if you see evidence that one of your team is a grabber, can you help them?

To succeed at self discipline, you must observe yourself and discover where you fail. Kelly McGonigal runs an incredibly popular public course out of Stanford University called 'The Science of Willpower'. She says we need to learn to 'observe ourselves with curiosity, not judgement'. A lot of her students are trying to quit smoking, lose weight, save money and achieve many of the things we all sometimes struggle with thanks to willpower scarcity.

Roy Baumeister moots self control as a metaphorical muscle that we can exercise and strengthen. Matthew Gaillot sees it as energy management. There's only so much willpower to go around. Wang and Dvorak's suggest that our brains treat energy like banks treat money. They'll let us have it for things we don't really need, but when we really need it they hang onto it for themselves. We have plenty of self control until we need it. Use it on something meaningless and there won't be enough left when you really need it. If you're forcing yourself to avoid chocolate all day, don't be surprised when you scream at your kids after work with less provocation than usual. It's a scarce resource - put your willpower where your goals are.

With Mischel's kids, the delayers managed their emotions by distracting themselves with other activities as if it were a game.

Mischel called this the 'strategic allocation of attention'. One of the grabbers' strategies was to focus on the cost of failure and they clearly found their strategy ineffective. Worrying about losing that second marshmallow just makes you think about marshmallows. This is called 'Ironic Reversal'. It's great that it has a name so you can think about that instead of whatever it is you're trying not to think about. We need to actively distract ourselves rather than vainly relying on logical instructions for our feeble conscious mind.

To make things worse, increases in brain activity spike the body's consumption of glucose for energy. Despite being not that big, our brain, even without promises of marshmallows or algebra, consumes 25% of our body's energy. That's why we have so many systems and heuristics to take the easy road. So while your brain is trying to not want a marshmallow, it could really use the calories. That's not ironic reversal, that's just ironic.

(My own doctor told me that a 1.5kg brain consumes as much energy as 30kg of muscle. This was after he asked me what I did for work and I said, 'Writing'. I suspect he was trying to make me feel better about not actually doing 'real work'.)

Before you can start helping your people increase their levels of self discipline, you're probably best to start with yourself. That's going to be a recurring theme in this book. You can train your willpower muscle according to Kelly McGonigal. Committing to small and consistent acts of self control can increase your overall levels of willpower in unrelated areas. For example, for a week, commit to saying, 'Yes,' instead of, 'Yeah'. It may seem unlikely but this will make a major difference in your life, though not because everyone starts thinking you are so much more eloquent.

What you're trying to coach your brain into is the habit of *noticing what it is you're about to do*. You get used to pausing before acting. That's a life-enhancing skill. Grabbing marshmallows is a primal instinct from the caveman days of genuine hunger and scarcity that is not only mostly unnecessary today but actually harmful. (Look out the window for evidence of the obesity epidemic.) Hunger is a threat and a stressor and, even though no grabber was actually hungry, it's the brain we're dealing with and not the stomach. We need to replace 'fight or flight' with 'pause and plan'.

Much of 'will' is 'skill'. Later, with Albert Bandura, Mischel re-ran the experiment with a variation. They had 'grabber' kids in with a 'delayer' adult. Many of the kids modelled the behaviours of the adult and taught themselves to delay. So, it seems that the ability to delay gratification, a critical success factor, is not something we're just born with. It can be taught and learned. That's good to know.

Mischel's conclusion was that the crucial skill was the 'strategic allocation of attention'. The delayers were able to deliberately distract themselves. When he and his colleagues taught children a simple set of mental tricks – such as pretending that the candy is only a picture, surrounded by an imaginary frame – he dramatically improved their self-control. The kids who hadn't been able to wait sixty seconds could now wait fifteen minutes. 'All I've done is given them some tips from their mental user manual,' Mischel says. 'Once you realize that will power is just a matter of learning how to control your attention and thoughts, you can really begin to increase it'.

Delay strategies require practice and support but it does work. For those trying to stop shopping, quit smoking or lose weight, other research has shown that avoidance is a failed strategy. Additionally, trying to repress thoughts about credit cards, cigarettes or cheesecake actually leads to a preoccupation with those exact things you're trying to avoid. Again, I strongly suggest checking out the YouTube video of Mischel's kids trying to not eat their marshmallow.

How can you help friends, family or your people at work enhance their self control?

A ten minute delay can give the hormone-rampaged subconscious enough time to flush itself out and let your sensible conscious brain, with your long-term interests at heart, get back in control. If you can engage people in questions for ten minutes at a time of self-control conflict that will help.

For those weight losers and smoke quitters, a better question is, 'How committed are you to your goal?' A less useful question is, 'How much progress do you think you have made?' Progress can often enable people to take some time off from their goal. If the conversation gets into issues of progress, always ask them if they remember *why* they're doing this.

Later on, we'll talk about how social proof and conformity

are strong drivers of people's behaviour. A study with the U.S. Air Force Academy tracked the fitness levels of 3,487 recruits over four years. Regardless of how fit they were when they arrived and where they were assigned, the best predictor of their final fitness levels was the fitness of the least fit cadet in their unit. That's social proof in action in a negative way but it's equally effective when used positively. If you, as a leader, can make self discipline and goal setting a normal and expected part of the way things are done around your workplace, the easier it'll be for everyone to achieve that for themselves personally.

DON'T EAT THE
MARSHMALLOW

It's just as well Mischel's studies were done when they were. They couldn't be done today, not with all the foods that kids are no longer allowed access to. God forbid little Timmy has a massive marshmallow-induced anaphylactic shock.

Brain-Based Boss Seed Of An Idea

Committing to small and consistent acts of self control can increase your overall levels of willpower in unrelated areas. For example, for a week, commit to saying, 'Yes', instead of, 'Yeah'. It seems unlikely to make a major difference in your life but it does and not because everyone starts thinking you are so much more eloquent. What you're trying to coach your brain into is the habit of noticing what it is you're about to do. You get used to pausing before acting. That's a life-enhancing, marshmallow-delaying skill.

Stop →Think →Act

What does self discipline mean for you personally? Were you a deferrer or a grabber? How has this helped or held you back?

Think of a particular person you lead? What clues do you see indicating they might be a deferrer or a grabber?

Thinking about a particular person you lead, how might you tweak your style to encourage them to be more self disciplined?

'Grit'

'I've never viewed myself as particularly talented. Where I excel is with a ridiculously sickening work ethic. While the other guy's sleeping, I'm working. While the other guy's eating, I'm working. While the other guy's making love, I'm making love too but I'm working really hard at it.' – Will Smith

Angela Lee Duckworth is a psychologist specialising in the study of achievement. In particular she's been looking for any predictors of people's long-term, meaningful achievement. Having talent is all well and good but what is the primary driver behind someone who realises that talent into success? Talent itself is not a predictor. The second most notable predictor seems to be self discipline, which we've covered already – don't eat the marshmallow. The primary driver, however, is a combination of stamina, sustained passion, perseverance, tenacity and doggedness. It's about not abandoning tasks from mere changeability or in the face of obstacles. She summarises these behaviours with the compelling word 'Grit'.

She studied successful people in a range of pursuits – musicians, teachers in under-resourced communities, spelling bee champions – but her most conspicuous study was of West Point Military Academy first year students. This period in their training is nick-named 'Beast Barracks' and not everyone who starts it finishes it. Each intake of recruits undergoes a battery of assessments early on, including checks for prohibited tattoos and

Duckworth's Grit Scale. They have a captive group, a range of variables to compare and a definite measure of success. The findings were consistent with her other studies. There was no correlation between talent going in and success, quite the reverse. There was an *inverse* relationship between talent levels going in and success. Self discipline was the second best predictor. The best predictor was Grit.

Another notable finding was that those with Grit isolate their weaknesses as they go and focus their deliberate practice on those areas. (I have a separate chapter later on about what they mean by 'Deliberate Practice'.) Grittier individuals had higher levels of education and made fewer career changes than less gritty peers of the same age.

You can check out Duckworth's scale online at www.authentichappiness.org. Do you finish everything you start or do your interests fluctuate from year to year?

A longitudinal study by Cathy Wylie, Hilary Ferral, Edith Hodgen, and Jean Thompson has been tracking the progress of hundreds of children through the New Zealand educational system. Its **findings** in 2011 reveal how the kids have achieved (or not) at NCEA – New Zealand's high school qualifications. Broadly speaking, they break down the participants into their strata of success and look at the associated characteristics within each band. What are the common traits of those who succeed versus those who don't (or, at least, haven't succeeded *yet*)?

The answer is *hard work*! Don't you hate it when your parents are right? I paraphrase, but the soft/people skills are more correlated to success than inherent braininess: Perseverance, curiosity, resilience. That's good news, as those are behavioural choices we can make and encourage our kids to make. It's not like 'tall'. That'd be a tough one. Though, if you manage to convert your short kid to tall, it may well prove their resilience!

I don't write about education. I write about improving results through engaging your people – employees, customers, whoever your people are. What do educational success factors have to do with that? Long gone now are the days, if they ever even existed, when we went to school and learnt, then left for a job and stopped learning. That kind of industrial revolution, people-as-cogs-in-the-machine thinking is archaic. Lifelong learning is the way of the future; it is the way of the now. Whatever machine you're operating today, whatever software you're an expert in today will be obsolete soon enough. Obsolescence is accelerating. The last company in the world (in India) that manufactured manual typewriters just got out of the typewriter manufacturing business. The number one ability needed for future is *the ability to learn.*

So, the factors driving academic success at high school are going to be needed after high school – in the workplace and in everyone's life outside work. Perseverance, curiosity, resilience can be taught and learnt and they can be recruited and supported in the workplace. I've heard for years the mantra from HR folk and managers in the hiring frame of mind, 'Hire attitude, train skill'. I mostly agree. This latest research certainly reinforces this philosophy of perseverance, curiosity and resilience. I bet it becomes even more important outside of school. Schools provide a lot of support and structure. The big bad world does not. People with perseverance, curiosity, resilience are far more likely to be these 'motivated, self starters' employers are always looking to hire. They're more likely to be the innovative entrepreneurs that our economies desperately need.

So, the next time you're hiring or looking to spend some training budget, give some researched-backed thought on the best way to invest that time, energy and money. Improved results and success are built with the building blocks of perseverance, curiosity, resilience. And maybe email the link to that news item about high school success to your kids. Or tweet it. Or send it by whatever means they're using today because they stopped using the previous latest best app because they found out *<u>you</u>* started using it...

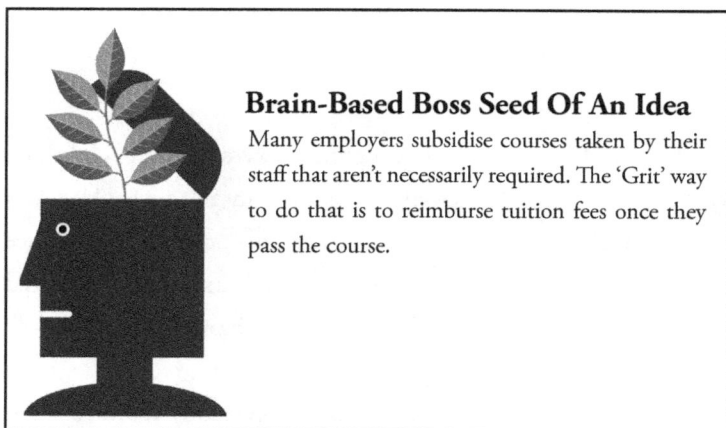

Brain-Based Boss Seed Of An Idea

Many employers subsidise courses taken by their staff that aren't necessarily required. The 'Grit' way to do that is to reimburse tuition fees once they pass the course.

Stop →Think →Act

What does this idea mean for you personally? To what extent have you displayed Grit?

What might this idea have to do with someone you lead?

Thinking about a particular person you lead, how might you tweak your style to encourage greater grit?

Mindset

You've probably got a fair idea that praise is a useful tool for leaders to influence behaviour but what, precisely, are you praising? Think back to the past few instances of praise you've delivered or received. Was it for some general and vague, 'Good job'? It's more effective if it's targeted to a specific behaviour and delivered as soon as practicable. But, again, what types of specific behaviour? Ideally, the behaviours you'd like reinforced and repeated. But, yet again, what are they? Let's come back to my stream of annoyingly pedantic questions.

Psychologist Carol Dweck, currently at Stanford University, ran studies on kids of a range of ages. They sat tests. Afterwards each received one of two statements of praise, either, 'Good job, you must be very smart,' or 'Good job, you must have worked very hard'. They were then told they needed to do another test, either one similar to the one they had just completed or one more challenging that could be fun to learn from. Most of the kids praised for 'being smart' opted for the easier test. 90% of those praised for 'working hard' opted for the challenge.

Then all the kids got another, more difficult, test. No one did very well. Dweck and her team observed that the group originally praised as 'smart' took it badly. The other group interpreted the result as them not having worked hard enough. A final test was given and this one was much on the same level of difficulty as the first. The group praised for being 'smart' did 20% *worse* than they did on the original test. The 'hard workers' did 30% *better*.

Dweck's famous finding from this and other studies was that people tended to fall into one of two groups. There are those who believe that their talents are a fixed trait. They believe they are or they aren't fast, strong, smart, etc. This is the *fixed mindset* group. Then there are those who believe that talent is something that can be developed. This is the *growth mindset* group. You can tell them apart by their behaviour towards work and mistakes. If you have a fixed mindset and believe you are what you are then why would you work hard and why would you attempt something new or challenging that could lead you to making mistakes and being judged on them? Growth mindset people do the work and see mistakes as a pathway to learning. They use the word 'yet' a lot. They say, 'I did' versus 'I am'. For them, becoming is better than being.

Once Dweck's kids were labelled as 'smart', their avoidance and dishonesty behaviours increased. To them, work is for those who don't have what it takes. Dweck says, 'Emphasising effort gives a child a variable they can control'. Emphasising natural talent takes it out of their control, makes image maintenance their primary concern and gives them no help in how to deal with failure. Fixed mindset people often give up. As we've already learned, the number one contributor to success is not giving up – gritty perseverance.

So, what?

In your work (and life) you want people who love challenge, believe in a connection between their effort and their results, and exhibit resilience in the face of (inevitable) setbacks. Praise effort not innate qualities. Dweck's research proves this.

Stop →Think →Act

What does this idea mean for you personally?

What might this idea have to do with someone you lead?

Thinking about a particular person you lead, how might you tweak your style to move them towards a growth mindset?

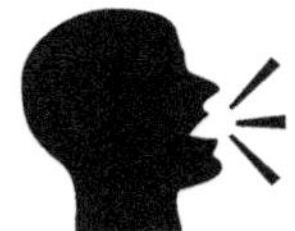

Optimism

Martin Seligman is renowned as the father of positive psychology. Prior to the past couple of decades, psychology was viewed by its practitioners as a means of helping people with problems and illnesses. That's great, thought Seligman, but couldn't it also be used to make the lives of people *without* mental problems or illnesses even better? Seligman and Mihaly Csikszentmihalyi (more about him very soon – including how to pronounce his name) stated in 1998 that the ambition of positive psychology was to build thriving in individuals, families, and communities. Not just helping the helpless but making the OK better.

Think about the people you lead at work. Where do you think each of them lie on a continuum between naturally optimistic and pessimistic? As you'll soon learn, that behaviour you're observing and judging as optimistic or pessimistic isn't natural at all. Height is a natural state, optimism is a choice.

When a negative event occurs, people choose how they react.

Pessimists tend to believe:	**Optimists tend to believe:**
The bad effects will be for a long time.	This is temporary.
This will undermine everything.	This is an isolated event.
This was my fault.	This is a challenge to learn from.

Look for evidence in the behaviour of the people you lead of the three Ps – permanence, pervasiveness and personalisation. Words are clues – always, never, everyone, every time, everything.

I'm not saying that optimism is always the right perspective and pessimism is always the wrong one. There are roles and situations where too much optimism can have negative results as can insufficient pessimism. Pessimists accurately judge how much control they have whereas optimists overestimate how much control they have. Overly optimistic people distort reality in a self-serving direction. Pessimists have a keener sense of reality. Mild 'professional pessimists' provide a sombre reality check and accuracy without too much self harm. It might pay to have one around to keep everyone else grounded. If the cost of failure is high, optimism is the wrong strategy.

It'll vary by role and situation but generally we're aiming for a balanced realism. Sales roles, for example, really need to be filled by optimists. You have to plan during your selection, placement and learning processes with this in mind. To what extent is persistence required amidst rejection, as in sales, or a keen sense of reality, as in a project accountant? Having said that, Seligman's research shows that people who are predominantly pessimistic end up less successful, less healthy and, by definition, less happy. They are more likely to get depressed easily. They achieve less than their talents warrant. Their beliefs promote inertia and become self-fulfilling. Their immune systems are less effective, contributing to higher genuine absences from work.

A common thought among the pessimistic population is,

'Nothing I do matters'. We'll learn later that the fundamental drivers of people's self motivation are autonomy, mastery and purpose. A person believing that nothing they do matters will never be self motivated. That very thought inhibits people from taking action. Ultimately, people with a long-term perceived absence of control over the outcome of their situation end up with mental illnesses. And even those who don't, experience significantly poorer performance at work and enjoyment of life. They certainly can't aspire to autonomy, mastery and purpose.

It's the way or style in which people think about the causes of successes and failures that determines, in the long run, who is a success or failure. This style is a learned habit. If you haven't hired or inherited people with this habit on their way in the door, it's your role as their leader to help them develop it. Cognitive psychologist Bernard Weiner described this as 'Attribution Theory'. Basically, people can choose to attribute responsibility to internal or external causes. If someone fails to operate software as instructed, they might think, 'I'm not smart enough,' or, 'I didn't try hard enough'. This links closely with the fixed versus growth mindset work of Carol Dweck we covered before. There's nothing they can do if they genuinely believe they're not smart enough. For those with a growth mindset, trying harder is a solution to not trying hard enough. That is a possibility so success is still a possibility.

A recurring theme throughout this book, above skill and natural talents, is that the primary traits for success for individuals and groups are resilience and perseverance. Clearly over-pessimism does not lend itself to resilience and perseverance. Even before encountering the research, I've always tried to instil not giving up into the workplaces I've lead, sports teams I've coached and my own children. I wish I'd had the tools provided by Seligman then. I'll pass them on to you shortly.

Through studies with dogs and electric shocks, which today are too cruel to detail here, Seligman showed that many of the dogs ended up helpless to stop their shocks even when they could. Opportunities to escape were presented but the dogs just sat and whined. They believed that nothing they did mattered even when circumstances changed. However, not all the dogs gave up. That's the important bit for us.

10% of the dogs gave up quickly. 60% of the dogs eventually ended up in a state of learned helplessness. But 30% of the dogs took action when it became available to them, improving their situation by stopping the shocks or escaping. What was so special about these 30%? Dogs are notoriously unreliable when it comes to completing and returning surveys, and people, despite what they think, cannot be assured of accuracy when reading a dog's mind. Fortunately similar studies have been conducted with people, firstly with babies, although not using electric shocks.

The ones who don't give up are ... *optimistic*. Resilience and perseverance contribute to success, and optimism is the foundation of resilience and perseverance. That's useful to know.

This gets us back to the question of what you as a leader in the workplace can do to instil optimism in firstly yourself then your team. Seligman promotes training people from pessimism to optimism. His technique is simple and memorable, which helps. However it is also quite a commitment as it aims to break habitual thought patterns.

Disputing your negative thoughts is a learned process. Negative thoughts drive unhelpful pessimistic behaviour such as inaction, and are often riddled with clue-words evoking permanence, pervasiveness and personalisation. Changing your interpretation of an event, asking yourself better questions and disputing your automatic beliefs will enable you to stay in the game, to continue to take action, to be empowered and engaged.

Seligman proposes a simple yet powerfully effective self-management 5-step technique for disputing your own negative thoughts:

A. Adversity
B. Belief
C. Consequence
D. Disputation (Argue with yourself sensibly)
E. Energization (Take some action)

Before you can coach your people in this technique, you need to practise it yourself. When an adversity occurs or something goes wrong or similar, what are your initial thoughts? To learn how to dispute your own automatic negative thoughts, you first have to listen to your own internal dialogue. One awareness technique is distancing. Externalising those negative voices in your head is useful. Imagine if it wasn't the voice in your head but a drunk in the street shouting at you. If that guy said those things to you, would you listen or give them any credence? Probably not, so why give any more weight to the drunk-guy-voice in your head? I've tried this. It works. It's mocking it and making it small or ridiculous.

Other awareness techniques include distraction. You've probably noticed a lot of people wearing rubber bands on their wrists these days. Some are idiots who think they have magnetic qualities which magically improve their energy. Some are supporters of causes or charities. But they can serve another purpose: when you get a pessimistic thought snap the rubber band back and ping yourself.

Think about your job. What is your 'wall'? What is the main task that makes you hesitate or shudder before forcing yourself to tackle it? For some, it might be making sales calls. What thoughts run through your head at that time, indicating your current beliefs?

'Disputation' is where you can make changes. Essentially you argue with yourself but in a rational and structured way. This takes committed practice and Seligman proposes a four-step process:

1. **Evidence**: Reality check. What are the facts? Put your detective hat on. List the proof for this belief. Prevent catastrophizing the adversity that has just happened and hunt out real evidence.
2. **Alternatives**: What might be all the possible factors that lead to the adversity? Concentrate on the ones that are short-term and precise rather than permanent and pervasive (for example, if you lost a sale, it might have been because you simply didn't stock what the customer

needed, rather than not being good at handling sales objections.) Ask yourself, 'Is there a less destructive way to look at this?'

3. **Implications**: If it turns out that your beliefs are valid, then the best course of action is to de-catastrophize. What does it imply? How probable is the worst-case scenario? For example, if you lost one sale, does that really imply the customer will never buy from you ever again?
4. **Usefulness**: Is the belief damaging? What's in it for me if I continue to hold this belief? What benefits are there for me if I change to a more useful belief? What would be a more useful belief? A good method is to list all the ways you can change for the future.

Let's look at an example from an individual leader's point of view trying to help themselves:

A. **Adversity**: One of my team just quit.

B. **Beliefs**: This happens all the time. I lack people skills. I only got promoted because of my good technical skills.

C. **Consequences**: I'm putting off hiring a replacement. That's a lot of effort and cost to bring someone in if they're not going to hang around for long.

D. **Disputation**: I have never asked why these people quit. It may have nothing to do with me. I should focus on things under my control.

E. **Energization**: Ask the remaining team members why they stay. Get them involved in recruiting a replacement.

Make exit interviews part of our process. Set some plans to spend time with new staff and interview them after three months on how it's going.

Let's look at an example from the point of view of a team leader trying to help their team work through Seligman's process:

A. **Adversity:** The boss has just declared that your team is merging with another.

B. **Beliefs:** You anticipate that people may react in different ways about this. Ask the individuals in your team what their thoughts and beliefs are about this proposed change. Write them down.

C. **Consequences:** Talk to your team individually and collectively about the consequences for them and the team if those with pessimistic beliefs continue to hold them. The change is going to happen. These could include sabotage or more passive-aggressive behaviour such as avoidance.

D. **Disputation:** Ask those with pessimistic beliefs about the current way of doing things. Was it perfect? Could it be improved? What are you basing your beliefs about the proposed changes on? Identify benefits of the changes relevant to them such as job security. Provide countering evidence or stories of similar changes that have worked for people like them. Provide a list of more helpful behaviours and thoughts they could have. (You might need this yourself if two teams are merging and the new bigger team will only need one leader ...)

E. **Energization:** Everyone needs to DO *something*. Pessimism feeds on, and is fed by, inertia. Helplessness results in inaction. Workplace environments undergoing restructure are fertile grounds for demotivators. You need to encourage people to take some action, almost any action, that can create in them a sense of influence over their situation and the changes being imposed from outside the team.

Brain-Based Boss Seed Of An Idea

Several companies I've worked with have included as the last part of their recruitment process a few hours of on-the-job exposure – not an assessment, not a simulation, actual time on-the-job buddied up with senior staff. Partly it is a chance to expose the applicant to the true nature of the job and gives them a chance to say, 'No'. But mostly it is a chance to expose the applicant to the eyes of the senior staff as they hit some obstacles and setbacks. This is highly revealing of their resilience and fixed or growth mindset at a time when its useful for the employer.

Stop →Think →Act

What does this idea mean for you personally?

What might this idea have to do with someone you lead?

Thinking about a particular person you lead, how might you tweak your style to promote appropriate levels of optimism?

Decision-Making

'Every thought on the wire leads to a fall.' –
Philippe Petit, High Wire Aerialist

People feel much more responsible for their actions than their inactions. Joseph Hallinan says, in his book *Errornomics – Why We Make Mistakes*, that at the moment you think you're making a decision, it only seems so. The point in time that you think that you're making a conscious and deliberate decision is an illusion. In reality, your subconscious has chosen for you much earlier.

In writing this book, I got to a point where I had a proof-reading deadline. I received the manuscript by email about 4pm on a Friday with a deadline of the following Monday morning. It was going to be a full-on weekend. At 4:37pm my laptop died. I had known that it was on its last legs and had been researching a new one. It's not a massive purchase these days but it's an important one that could annoy me and cost me if I chose poorly. I'd even scribbled up a little grid on paper showing dozens of various models comparing what I thought were their critical specifications. I had definitely decided that I would buy a new laptop but I hadn't decided when or which one. The 'when' had now been decided for me and I had twenty-three minutes to decide the 'which'.

I decided in a heartbeat and have had zero regrets. My subconscious mind had been processing for a while. I made a good decision and, more importantly, I *felt good* about it. More about regret minimisation later.

Most days are made up of a series of decisions, like which of three cereals should you have for breakfast or which task should you start next. Some decisions might be whether to buy a house or signing a contract to undergo elective surgery. Maybe you agonise over every decision or just the big ones or none at all? The rest you just go with your gut feeling. Sometimes you'll regret the decisions you make, or choose not to make. What's the smartest way to make decisions or help others make them? It depends on the complexity of the decision.

Ap Dijksterhuis, out of the University of Amsterdam, conducted several studies on just this subject. However, like many of the researchers I've read for this book, they've used sentences like, 'Because of the low processing capacity of consciousness, conscious thought was hypothesized to be maladaptive when making complex decisions'. And they're right but wordy. In my words, it's hard to think about a bunch of complicated things at once.

You might like to imagine you're a rational, logical person who'll weigh up the pros and cons of each decision, especially the big ones, and make the best decision you can with the information you have. But what Dijksterhuis found was quite different. He studied consumers and shoppers in lab conditions and in actual sales situations – during and after. The 'after' is especially important, as that is when the true quality and impact of a decision hit home.

All participants were facing a purchase decision of varying sizes. Half were interrupted and distracted during their decision-making process. All were subsequently followed up on how they felt about their decision post-purchase. The thinking was that the distraction allowed the unconscious mind, which can handle lots of complexity at once, to process the decision. It hooks into the brain's emotional centres. This is where 'gut feelings' may come from. Plus emotional responses to the choices are pre-rehearsed and emotional responses to each decision are assessed by your brain with you not consciously aware of them.

His findings were that, 'simple choices (such as between different towels or different sets of oven mitts) indeed produce better results after *conscious thought*, but that choices in complex matters (such as between different houses or different cars) should be left to *unconscious thought*. Named the 'deliberation-without-attention' hypothesis, it was confirmed in four studies'.

Conscious thought focuses attention on whatever factors manage to squeeze themselves into our limited conscious mind at the time. That distorts perception and can over-inflate the relative importance of certain factors.

Researcher Loren Nordgren joked about Rene Descartes' famous quote, 'I think therefore I am'. That was all well and good but was he always happy with the shoes he chose to buy? Overthinking doesn't make for good decisions when it's not a simple decision.

I'm not suggesting that lack of attention is a good thing. Otherwise we may as well put teenagers in charge of all the important decisions. Most can usually (always) be relied upon to provide the 'without attention' component! No, it has to be a bit more structured than that.

Both studies look at what might be called intentional self distraction. They contrasted three approaches to decision-making: make an instant choice, long list of pros and cons, briefly distracting the conscious mind. The latter was the most effective and, down the road a bit, evoked the least regret.

If you just skim read Malcolm Gladwell's book *Blink*, you might assume that instant decisions are often the best. But on closer examination, I reckon Gladwell agrees with Dijksterhuis. Both reject the supposedly time-tested tradition of logically weighing up, over a period of intense concentration, a list of pros and cons. It takes ages and delivers a poorer result.

My shorthand version of a useful process is:

1. Introduce the problem and range of solution options.
2. Carry out a pre-set 3 minute distraction activity.
3. Return to the problem and/or the options. Make your choice.
4. Live with it.

So, what?

I had it drummed into me, and I subsequently preached to those I trained, the commonsense of structured event interviewing as a tool for recruiting. I was schooled on the value of decision matrix spreadsheets when evaluating complex contract tender responses. Does this research mean those formal processes have no value? No. Recruiting and big contracts are expensive and the consequences of mistakes are significant. At the very least, you may need to retrospectively justify your decision (ie cover your butt). I think the lesson of deliberation-without-attention is that it pays to try both approaches. If they don't match, you might need to do some more research and ask some more questions.

Stop →Think →Act

What does this idea mean for you personally?

What might this idea have to do with someone you lead?

Thinking about a particular person you lead, how can you introduce them to trying different ways of making decisions, including deliberation without attention?

Anchoring And Adjustment

Amos Tversky and Daniel Kahneman have done several studies on the heuristic where people overly and disproportionately rely on one piece of information (or 'anchor') when making a decision or engaging in a behaviour. Once the anchor is set, there is a bias toward adjusting or interpreting other information to reflect the anchored information. Through this cognitive bias, the first information learned about a subject can affect future decision-making. (Warning to those averse to the touchy feelies – many anchors originate in your childhood. Thanks Mum.)

Kahneman writes of a study done at the San Francisco Exploratorium. Visitors were surveyed about their guesses of the height of the world's tallest redwood tree. They were each asked two questions. The first question varied. It was either, 'Is the height of the world's tallest redwood tree more or less than 1200 feet?' or 'Is the height of the world's tallest redwood tree more or less than 180 feet?'

However, the *second* question was always, 'What's your best guess of the height of the world's tallest redwood tree?' The table below shows how the anchor in the first question (180ft and 1200ft) influenced the respondent's average guess in feet.

Anchor In Their First Question	Average Guess In Feet
1200	844
180	282

Clearly there is anchoring and adjustment going on, but how great is the effect? The difference between the two average guesses is 562 (=844-282). The difference between the two anchors is 1020 (=1200-180). 562 divided by 1020 is 55%. That's the significant anchoring effect in this instance. Another study looked at whether the original listing price for houses in the real estate market affected an expert's assessment of the houses' actual market values. Because researchers like a laugh as much as the next person, they studied a group of real estate agents versus a control group of random students with zero housing experience. The anchoring effect for the students was 48%. The anchoring effect for the realtors was 41%. The delightful conclusion wasn't just in those numbers. When told of their results and then having the anchoring effect explained to them, the students accepted it. The realtors, however, vehemently denied there was an anchoring effect. That kind of close-mindedness does not lend itself to personal or professional development and long-term success. You might want to bear that in mind yourself.

Feedback is important here. Realtors don't get much feedback and it's a long time coming. 'Calibration' is the balance between your real and perceived abilities. Young male drivers, on average, have very poor calibration between their real and perceived driving abilities. They are long gone from much of the mayhem they cause, thus avoiding feedback until it's too late. According to Joseph Hallinan, weather forecasters have excellent 'calibration'. The reason for this is the quantity and quality of feedback they get. Everyone is willing and able to let weather forecasters know when they're wrong.

Stop →Think →Act

What does this idea mean for you personally?

What might this idea have to do with someone you lead?

Thinking about a particular person you lead, how can you increase the frequency of their calibration and open their minds to the anchors from their past biasing their current decisions?

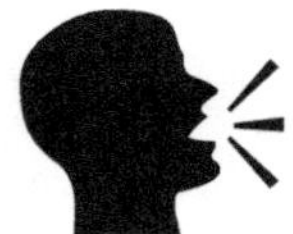

Realism

Thomas Gilovich found that 94% of university professors believe themselves to be an above average professor. (I presume they weren't math professors.)

David Armor and Shelley Taylor found that MBA students wildly over-estimate their future job and salary prospects; financial analysts over-estimate corporate earnings; and smokers believe themselves to be much less likely to suffer from smoking-related disease than other smokers. I did my own survey at weddings. 100% of briders and grooms, on their wedding day, declared they believed their marriage would last forever. In reality, 50% of marriages end in divorce.

The Amygdala is the brain's emotion centre. Imaging studies have shown that when people recall actual past negative events, the Amygdala strongly lights up. But when asked to anticipate those same type of events as future occurrences, the Amygdala barely lights up. There isn't the emotional connection and reinforcement so there isn't the behavioural influence over us.

Think about unrealistic optimism as you drive to work tomorrow on the roads filled with the 80% of drivers you believe to be less skilled than yourself.

Brain-Based Boss Seed Of An Idea

One company I worked with had a mandatory inclusion in all their project plans for projects over a specified value they considered to be 'major'. All stakeholders needed to attend and actively participate in what they called a 'Pre-Mortem'. Unlike a 'Post-Mortem' where experts determine the cause of death after a person has died, the 'Pre-Mortem' was conducted by project managers before the project got the final sign-off. Experts and non-experts alike operate in the meeting as if the project had already failed and examine why in an attempt to pre-empt and mitigate problems.This was a simple, effective and practical way to address most people's inherent unrealistic optimism.

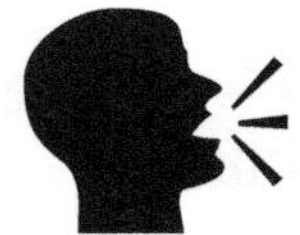

Attention

People have a tendency to remember incomplete tasks better than completed ones. It's called the Zeigarnik effect after Soviet psychologist Bluma Zeigarnik who first studied it. She had been out to dinner with her professor (I'm not judging anyone man) and he'd made a point that the waiting staff could remember details of orders that had yet to be paid but couldn't remember the paid orders. It was as if, once the order was paid for, the waiter's brain ticked a box and dumped the information it believed it no longer needed. Fair enough too, as it probably needed the limited space in its conscious memory for other things. I know mine would.

This is certainly an argument that supports the taking of breaks rather than ploughing ahead to fully complete a task regardless of how productive you're feeling at the time.

We remember unsolved problems, frustrations, failures and rejections much better than our successes and completions.

However, the Zeigarnik effect is not just remembering incomplete tasks better than completed ones. In 2008, Roy Baumeister and Brad Bushman found that this effect also included the intrusion of incomplete tasks into our conscious mind, interrupting what we're currently trying to think about. The upside of this effect is that it improves memory. The downside is that it can increase anxiety. Anxiety is a stressor which is either a good or a bad thing, depending on what you do about it, and the frequency and duration of the physiological stress response.

So, a technique for anyone in your team for whom procrastination is a drag on their life is for them to, at least, make a start and let the Zeigarnik effect nag their subconscious into action.

Stop →Think →Act

What does this idea mean for you personally?

What might this idea have to do with someone you lead?

Thinking about a particular person you lead, how might you tweak your style in dealing with them to be more effective?

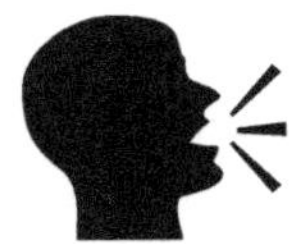

Ineffective Behaviours

You know these people. They brag or drop names or come on too strong or show off or dominate conversations. It never works but they continue to do it anyway and irritate those around them in the process. Why do they persevere with such ineffective behaviour?

They keep behaving like that because of a lack of feedback. Few, if any, people have ever let them know the impact their behaviour has on others and its ineffectiveness. They get ignored and avoided. Therefore no alternative strategies ever get used, practised or experienced by them. They continue with their existing behaviour because, even with the little success they have had with it, it has at least worked sometimes and that is better than never.

Their leaders in the workplace need to get them to try other approaches in incremental steps to, at least, get some experience and opportunity or feedback and success. It goes without saying that the leader needs to generate some feedback. Ironic, given that 'going without saying' is the problem in the first place.

The Dunning-Kruger Effect reveals a surprisingly inverse relationship between how good people *think* they are at something and how good they *actually* are at it. Low skilled people suffer from illusions of superiority. In 1999 Justin Kruger and David Dunning from Cornell University released their results of a series of studies on people's self assessment of their abilities at humour, logical reasoning and grammar, compared to their actual skill levels.

Before we get all judgemental about these people, the highly skilled are also very bad at assessing their own relative skill levels, except they *underestimate* it. If they find a task easy many of them tend to assume others do so too. The inaccuracy of the low-skilled stems from a mistake about *themselves.* The inaccuracy of the highly-skilled stems from a mistake about *others.* If you're highly-skilled and you're supposed to be leading others, this is just as big a problem as the delusions of grandeur of the lesser-skilled.

The more skills you have, the more practice you've put in, and the more experiences you've had, the more able you are to compare yourself to others. You learn your gaps. In comparing yourself to real experts, you become very aware of those gaps. For the as-yet-unskilled, one solution for you as a leader is to expose them to more relevant experiences – 'time on ball' as soccer coaches say. Stage time. Flying hours. And, of course, that creates extra opportunities for feedback which you need to make sure happens.

So, what? It seems a critical first step in developing skill at anything is an awareness that you need to. They should hand out a one-pager on the Dunning-Kruger Effect to those auditioning for *American Idol.* Except, of course, those who most needed it wouldn't realise they did. As opposed to high performers, poorer performers do not learn from feedback suggesting a need to improve. I'm sure the *American Idol* judges would agree with that.

Stop →Think →Act

What does this idea mean for you personally?

What might this idea have to do with someone you lead?

Thinking about a particular person you lead, how might you, regardless of their level as a performer, ensure they get enough accurate feedback on that level of performance, even when you're not around?

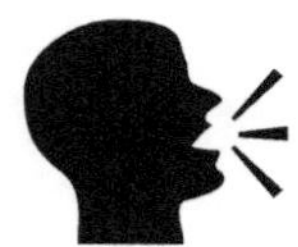

Principle 2: Mastery

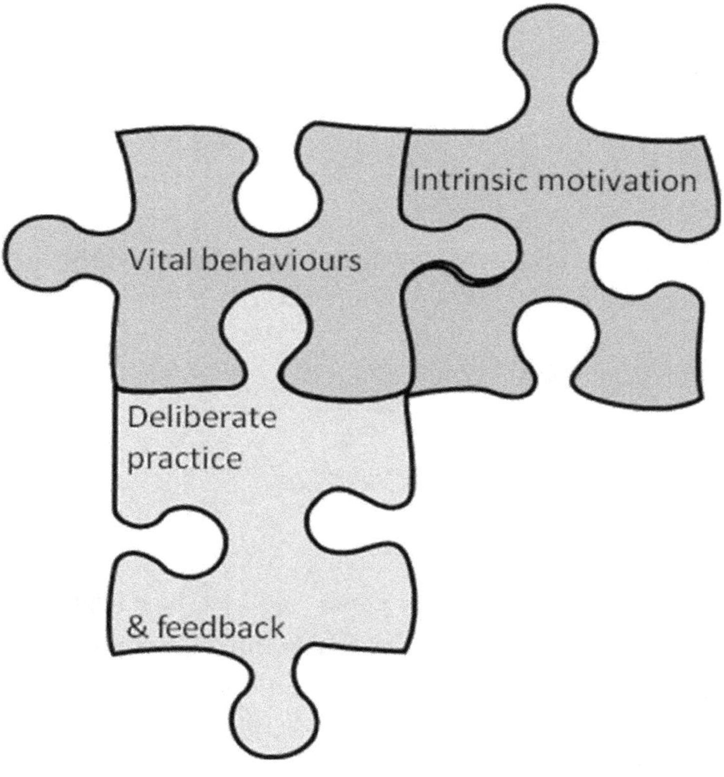

Intrinsic motivation

Vital behaviours

Deliberate practice & feedback

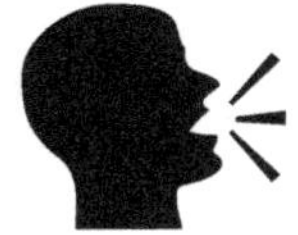

'Flow'

Hungarian psychologist Mihaly Csikszentmihalyi once lamented that society has plenty of one-minute managers and not enough 100-year managers. Aside from deep witticisms about management and a famously difficult-to-pronounce surname (it's pronounced 'cheeks sent me high') he is most renowned as the developer of the concept of 'Flow'. Flow is a mental state in which a person, in the process of an activity, is fully immersed in a feeling of energized focus and full involvement. You're 'in the zone baby'. It happens sometimes by random chance and it's a powerfully productive state. What can leaders do to promote it within themselves and their teams?

They say time flies when you're having fun. Think back to a time for you at work when time flew. What were you doing?

When we are fully engaged, dopamine surges through our brain. Dopamine acts as a neurotransmitter and it has many functions in the brain, including important roles in behaviour and cognition, voluntary movement, motivation, punishment and reward, sexual gratification, sleep, mood, attention, working memory, and learning.

Csikszentmihalyi's conclusions about 'Flow' won't surprise you. They're similar to what many of the other researchers we've covered have found. People enjoy doing their best and contributing to something beyond themselves. The twin concepts of differentiation and integration: You are a unique individual yet you belong to a group or shared purpose. Listen when people ask your staff what they do. There's a big difference between, 'I lay bricks,' and, 'I'm helping build a cathedral'. In organisations, a person lucky enough to be in a state of 'Flow' will be experiencing:

- Clear goals.
- Immediate feedback.
- A balance between opportunity and capacity (a high level of challenge AND a high level of skill).
- Deep concentration.
- The present is what matters.
- Control is no problem.
- The sense of time is altered.
- A loss of ego.

You can't be in 'Flow' all the time. No one can. No one should try. Everyone is a constant flux all the time as challenge varies and their skill needs of each situation change. As you can see from the diagram below, 'Flow' is just one of the states we can experience given the relative combination of challenge and skill for us as individuals in any given task.

People's States Are Influenced By The Balance Between Skill And Challenge.

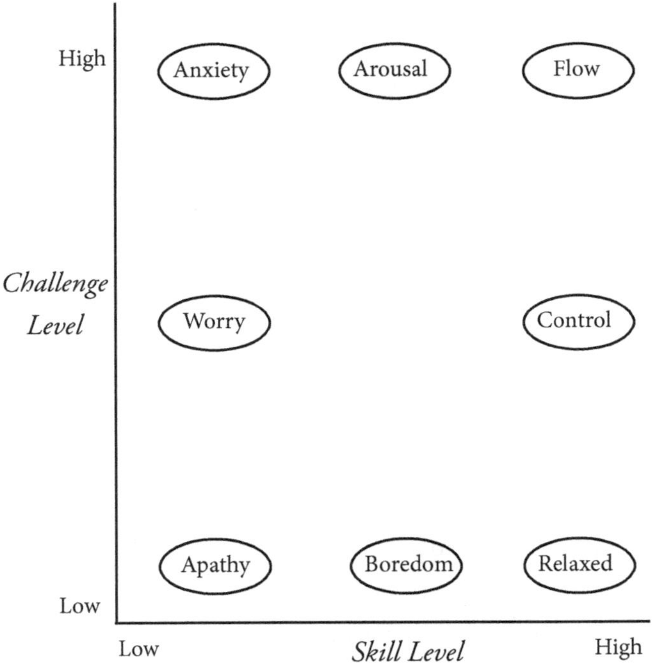

The diagram below succinctly presents the challenge leaders face in trying to support a 'flow-friendly' workplace. Everybody's different. Everybody changes. It's even more challenging than this diagram suggests. More realistically, the circles should be constantly moving but I couldn't work out how to do that, not even in an e-book. I'm not saying it's so difficult that you shouldn't try. I'm just trying to sprinkle some realism dust on your expectations.

As a leader, you need to put your people into situations where they have reasonably, but not overly challenging, goals, frequent feedback and multiple levels of achievement. If you're training a new person on-the-job, break down the tasks so they can get a continual sense of progression.

Part of 'Flow' is concentrating on a task. Gloria Mark from the University of California extensively studied worker interruptions. On average, workers were interrupted from their task every 185 seconds. Switching tasks within a subject area isn't so bad but it is across subjects. The average time for this is every ten and a half minutes. Oddly, half of these interruptions were 'self-interruptions'. I'm guessing many of these workers weren't neuro-surgeons or air traffic controllers so maybe it isn't life or death, but how much potential for inefficiency and errors is there in having to work out where you left off and recollecting your thoughts hundreds of times a day? For no reasons visibly obvious or discernable to the researchers, people would stop what they were doing and do something else, then go back to the original task. So, as a leader, we should try and create an environment conducive to people getting into 'Flow' as often as they can.

According to Mark, 82% of interrupted work is returned to on the same day but that original primary task isn't returned to, on average, until twenty three minutes and fifteen seconds later. Your brain has to do a lot of double handling to get back to where it was and that's inefficient and tiring. Plus there's the chance of error by omission. Let's not even worry about the business for a moment. What is the cost to the person? Mark cites stress, frustration and unnecessary effort.

Multi-tasking is a convenient and egocentric delusion. There is no such thing as dividing attention between two conscious activities. If you think you're doing several things 'at once' you're not. Even if you're good at juggling multiple things, you're not simultaneously maintaining attention in your conscious mind on more than one thing. You're not multi-tasking, you're task-switching. That's do-able but has a major drag effect on efficiency and quality. It also sucks the energy out the brain like, well, you know what it's like.

Interestingly, Mark, whose very job is studying worker interruptions and how to protect productive time, was asked how she copes with it herself. Her response, 'I stay home...'.

In 2012, Ernst & Young's 'Productivity Pulse Survey' in New Zealand estimated that such interruption wastage accounted for 15 – 21% of work time causing a nineteen billion dollar drag on the nation's economy. That roughly equates to one working day each week being wasted. The three biggest villains are unnecessary emails, waiting for management approvals and technology malfunctions. Though to be fair, emails don't send themselves do they? And they don't put a gun to your head and make you read them. Do they? People get distracted. Management needs to take action about the red tape and the unreliable systems but individuals need to manage their own responses to those email dings.

Daniel Kahneman notes that one outwardly visible symptom of mental effort is dilation of the pupil of the eye. He devised a little optometrist-like contraption for his participants to pop their heads in during observed and videoed activities. In one activity, they were shown a flash card with a 4-digit number and they had to quickly add one to each of the number's digits. For example, 5294 becomes 6305. It's not rocket science but you have to think about it. He found that switching from one task to another, especially under time pressure, is effortful. No surprises there. Anything you can do, as a leader, to reduce cognitive strain is a good thing.

Why are we so easily distracted? Why, when we're on a deadline to write a book, do we see the little flashing email icon in the corner and simply must go see what it is 'in case it's important'? Clearly, in my sad case, going and checking my email gives me something positive to look forward to, even if I don't know what it is. For my brain, it's a treat as much as any marshmallow. I know I shouldn't but I do. Where's that famous willpower of mine to save the day?

Psychologist Roy Baumeister ran a study at the University of Kentucky using carrots and candy. There were two groups of subjects. Individuals from each group had before them a plate of candy and a plate of carrots. One group could touch the candy but not the carrots while the other group could touch the carrots but not the candy. After a time, both groups were tested on almost impossible anagram puzzles to measure how long they persisted. (Remember, perseverance is one of the primary drivers of success.) The group who'd been allowed the candy, and therefore hadn't had to tap into their willpower reserves to repress their candy-grabbin' urges, were significantly more persistent on the puzzles. If we have to force ourselves to do or not do something, we're less able to do so for whatever challenge is next.

From this he concluded that people start their days with a certain amount of self control that gets consumed through our deliberate acts of self control. These acts can include:

- Suppression of thoughts (think of anything except polar bears).
- Suppressing urges (I NEED to check my email).
- Having multiple conflicting goals.
- Hiding something.

How does the expert suggest we refill our willpower tank if we spend a lot of our time repressing thoughts, urges and keeping secrets? Plan A seems to be avoiding situations that will deplete your willpower in the first place. Hide those temptations. Remove myself from that flashing email icon's presence or deactivate that function. The other suggestions imply a genuine psychological-physiological connection: eat a small amount of real sugar, exercise regularly and avoid alcohol. (I think instinctively we all knew that last one was coming.) Daniel Kahneman writes of a study of Israeli parole judges. In their process, the default decision is to reject parole applications. Approvals require the judges to argue it out and come to a considered justification. The average rate of approval is 35%. In the hour following meal breaks, the average rate of approval is 65%. Seriously, whoever you're dealing with at work, in whatever context, try not to do it before lunch.

I mentioned polar bears before for a reason. Baumeister is famous for another study (and before him, Dan Wegner) where he asked a class to think of anything except polar bears but if they should happen to think of a polar bear then they should ring a little bell he'd given to each of them. The classroom's airwaves were awash with ringing within seconds. This effect is called 'Ironic Reversal'. Variations on this study have been conducted over the years proving that if you want someone not to panic then the worst thing you can say is, 'Don't panic.' You'd be better off saying something like, 'Remain calm'. Saying, 'Don't spill the milk,' to a child or, 'Don't look down,' to a trainee tightrope walker would be equally counter-productive. And counter-productive is something they teach you to avoid at tightrope-walking school. Don't tell your people what *not to do*, tell them what *to do*. (Obviously that last sentence contradicted itself. I'm not proud of that.)

Brain-Based Boss Seed Of An Idea

Some companies allocate a specified proportion of time where staff can work on whatever they like. 3M is famous for doing this years ago resulting in, amongst other things, the invention of Post-It Notes.

Stop →Think →Act

What does this idea mean for you personally?

What might this idea have to do with someone you lead?

Thinking about a particular person you lead, how effective are they at maintaining attention, avoiding distraction and remaining on-task? What can you do about the causes if they're not?

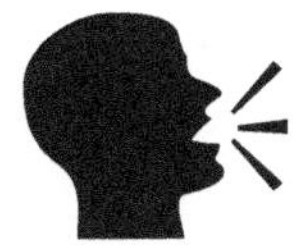

Effective Coaching And Natural Learning

W. Timothy Gallwey writes about not being able to master, or even really enjoy, anything until self interference in the mind is dealt with. Tennis is his primary metaphor and he writes about the 'inner game' in our minds between two players he calls 'Self 1' and 'Self 2'. They remind me a bit of the troublesome imps in *The Cat In The Hat*. Although it's only Self 1 who can be labelled as troublesome, spouting dialogue that prevents people from fulfilling their potential. You're about to hit the ball or make the call or approach the customer and the little voice of Self 1 says, 'Don't screw this up,' or 'Be sure to use their name'. After you've hit the ball, made the call or approached the customer, the little voice of Self 1 says, 'That was great!' or 'I think you mispronounced their name'. Self 2 is that quieter, instinctive voice of actual experience rather than critical judgements.

Is that inner dialogue familiar to you? Do you think it goes on in the minds of the people you're trying to lead about their work? Do you think it helps? (The answers are yes, yes and no.)

Learning is retarded in conditions of high anxiety and low acceptance. If you've got kids, maybe they're at a stage when they're learning to walk. If you haven't got kids, most of you would have learned to walk quite some time ago (even if you've pretty much given it up recently). No one gives parents a lesson plan on teaching their kid to walk and when the child falls down, no supervisor shouts, 'Well, that is not going to look good on your performance review!' There is trust in our capacity to learn from our own experience. That's *natural learning*. Learning is from the inside-out not the outside-in and the responsibility for the learning lies with the learner. Contrast that with the *forced mode* of teaching, coaching and supervision commonplace in schools and workplaces. You'll recognise some aspects, perhaps even from yourself? There are 'should' and 'shouldn't' directions, implying that there is 'one right way'. Change is a movement from 'bad' to 'good' as assessed by a third party. The cycle of self interference's internal dialogue is mirrored with Self 1's commanding and judgemental commentary.

Think back to the section of deliberation without attention. A coach or supervisor gives you well-meaning advice, maybe even specific instructions, but the conscious mind can only handle so much at once. The coach or supervisor doing this is as bad as Self 1. What the coach on the court, or you in your workplace, needs to do is distract your people from their own internal chatter and allow them to engage their unconscious mind in natural learning. But how?

Just like deliberation without attention, a distraction is needed but you don't need to go off and play a word puzzle for three minutes in the middle of your tennis game or your sales call. The key is to focus on a specific detail of what's happening – a neutral but critical variable. Gallwey spoke of listening to the sound of the ball as the racquet struck it. Rather than obsess about foot placement and speed and angles and dozens of other minor and complex variables, just listen for the sound, observe the result and let your unconscious mind work out what behaviour led to the best outcome as you continue to practise.

Winton Bates wrote about how he used Gallwey's process to lessen his stuttering. Having a coach or Self 1 say, 'Don't hit it near the baseline' is akin to saying, 'Think of anything except a polar bear'. It's inherently self-defeating. 'Don't look down', Don't panic', 'Don't spill the milk', and similar commands tend to lead to exactly the outcome you were hoping to avoid. Bates' observed that his speech was especially prone to blocking when he was thinking, 'Don't block'. ('Don't stutter' is about as useful a thought in your head as, 'Don't look down'.) He learnt to distract himself by focusing on listening to a particular detail of how he sounded as he spoke. His unconscious mind did the rest once Self 1 shut the hell up and let Self 2 use its superior cognitive processing ability.

When I wrote earlier about learning being retarded in conditions of high anxiety and low acceptance, you might have wondered if I was accusing you of being a leader who's causing those things. Even if you were, and I'm sure you're not, that wouldn't be the worst thing. It's worse when those things are caused by the voices in people's own heads. Not the voices that say, 'Look both ways before you cross the street though'. That's useful. Listen to that one.

So, what?

Resistance to change is often resistance to the process of change rather than the change itself. As a leader in your workplace, trying to generate conditions conducive to natural learning Gallwey would tell you that A.C.T.: **A**wareness, **C**hoice and **T**rust are his platforms to improved performance. We have talked about 'Awareness' by using the technique of focusing on a specific detail of what's happening – a neutral but critical variable. 'Choice' is about keeping as much choice with the learner as possible. 'Trust' is about relying on the unconscious mind of the learner and not reverting to the old command and judge coaching approach at the first sign of problems. Your role is to ask questions to help clarify their goals, connect to their pre-existing intrinsic motivations, separate the person from their behaviour and bring them back away from the Self 1 voice in their heads. What obstacles do you need to remove – boredom, stress, feeling patronised?

Again, open-questioning is a great technique for this. To milk the tennis metaphor one last time, if you, as an experienced tennis coach, knew that what needs to happen is for the learner to keep their eye on the ball, you could simply tell the learner to, 'Keep your eye on the ball'. A more effective approach would be to ask an open question that they could only answer if they had in fact been watching the ball. What question would you ask?

I've asked people in workshops and very few people get close to the right type of question. Some ask, 'Did you watch the ball?' That's a closed question but it is also dripping with judgement. It's very Self 1.

You might have a better one but the best I've found is, 'At what spot on the ball does your racquet connect?' It's non-judgemental, distracting from Self 1; it is a neutral but critical variable and can only be answered by watching the ball. It doesn't actually matter if you hit a fuzzy yellow bit of the ball or the *W* in *Wilson* but it does matter that you watch the ball.

You're probably not a tennis coach. Maybe you'd like your new person to stack lettuces properly or upsell power tools in a building supply warehouse. What questions can you ask them in your workplace?

Much of what I've been writing about revolves around the theme of humans having many natural psychological tendencies and the folly of trying to fight or ignore these rather than working with them. Nowhere is this more vivid than when it comes to teaching, training and coaching others, or, as I prefer to frame it, *helping others to learn.*

Gallwey's underlying premise is that learning is retarded in conditions of high anxiety and low acceptance. What causes high anxiety and low acceptance in a learning context?:

- Trying hard to change (Remember, the brain prefers effortlessness).
- A teaching method that states or implies that there is 'one right way' and compares what you're doing to that ideal method with a series of 'should' and 'shouldn't' commands.
- Change as a movement from 'bad' to 'good' as judged by a third party.

I thought to myself, as I read Gallwey's words, that I remember having bosses who taught me like that and then I knew that I'd been a boss like that myself sometimes. But then it got interesting. Often the judgmental third party telling you that you're good or bad and that you should or shouldn't do things is... YOU. That struck a chord with me – the cycle of mental self-interference.

Think back to your first job. Maybe you waited tables. Think back to learning to drive, or play a musical instrument, or play a sport. Recall a time when you attempted a task you were trying to improve at. Was there that little voice in your head? Did it give you 'should' and 'shouldn't' commands? After you did the task, did it verbally pat you on the back or slap you in the face?

What's the solution to the unhelpful inner voice of what Gallwey calls 'Self 1'? It's the power of non-judgemental awareness. Distract yourself from Self 1 by focusing on a specific detail of what's happening as it happens. Ideally it should be a neutral but critical physical variable. Using tennis as an example, you might focus on watching exactly where on the tennis ball your racquet makes contact. It's physical, observable, emotionally neutral and critical. That focus distracts you from Self 1 telling you something like, 'Straighten your wrist'. Conscious commands are limited in their usefulness compared to the lightning speed of the subconscious. Distract Self 1 and your wrist straightening worries will take care of themselves.

If your workplace isn't a tennis court, maybe the scenario is a sales call and the wrist straightening is objection handling. What might be the specific, observable, neutral and critical variable you could observe? I'd listen to the exact words and phrases the customer uses in their objection. I'd write them down to make sure I used those exact words myself when replying. They'll give great clues on how to handle it and the focus of listening intently will shut up Self 1.

As Gallwey says, conscious acceptance of oneself and one's actions *as they are* frees up the incentive and capacity for spontaneous change. Pay attention to the technique without making a conscious effort to change the technique. Learn from the inside-out not the outside-in. Natural learning lasts when it's allowed to work whereas forced learning is unreliable. Natural learning relies on awareness, choice and trust. Other tips for leaders trying to help those they lead to learn include:

- The responsibility for learning lies with the learner.
- Keep choice with the choice-maker ('What do <u>you</u> want to improve on today?').
- Coach them to clarify their own goals and their own motivation as best they can.
- Separate them from their behaviour.
- Resistance to change is often resistance to the process of change rather than the change itself.
- Identify major internal obstacles (call centre operators often report boredom, stress and feeling patronised for example.)

Does this sound familiar? Choice is another word for an aspect of autonomy, a basic human psychological need. Focus is a critical part of 'Flow' and focus is easy to sustain if someone is doing something they have chosen to do. Desire drives focus.

Stop →Think →Act

What does this idea mean for you personally?

What might this idea have to do with someone you lead?

Thinking about a particular person you lead, what open questions can you ask them to prime their Self 2 voice during their work? What are their neutral but critical variables?

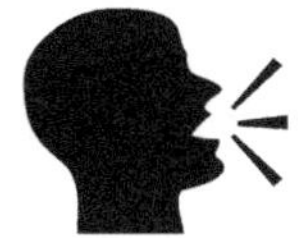

Feedback

Psychologist Marcial Losada's 1999 study looked at communication in teams, particularly the ratio of positive to negative statements. Various teams were tagged as being high, medium or low performing based on profitability, customer satisfaction and evaluations from management. The lowest performing teams had a ratio of positive to negative statements of 2.9013:1. (For us non-academics, let's round that to 3:1.) The highest performing teams averaged around 6:1. But there were diminishing returns and eventually a negative effect. Some of the worst performing teams had an 11:1 ratio so everyone must have been so busy hugging and bestowing warm fuzzies on everyone else, that no one ever did any actual productive work. That level of positivity is over-the-top, unrealistic and evidently not productive.

What's so special about this magical zone of positivity? Losada says a highly connected team balances internal and external focus while also balancing enquiry and advocacy. If you've ever been in a highly negative workplace, you'll know what he's talking about. If you make a mistake and get slapped with blame and negativity, that drives the behaviours of avoidance and defensiveness.

Ori and Rom Brafman conducted studies on participants who had their brains scanned as they took part in an electronic ball toss game with a computer. At various points, the computer 'rejected' them. Even from an inanimate machine, this act of rejection caused the participants' brains' anterior cingulate cortexes to activate. This is the brain's centre associated with physical pain. It's also been referred to as, 'The Oh Shit Circuit'.

Have you ever had a back spasm, toothache, migraine and tried to work through it? How'd that work out for you? Not great, I bet. Even if you managed to struggle through, how did it affect your concentration and interrelationships with those around you? Remember, according to Losada, we need a high positive:negative statement ratio. That's not likely when you're in pain or your brain thinks you are because it can't differentiate between actual physical pain and emotional rejection.

It doesn't even have to be an act of proactive rejection by a boss, colleague or customer. The Brafmans found that 'social isolation' can generate the same response. This has implications for those of you leading teams that are separated geographically or between shifts. Being alone for extended periods reduces mental acuity. Connecting genuinely with other people makes you smarter, healthier and more productive.

We covered the brain's mirror neurons earlier with talk of research assistants stealing the monkey's peanuts. When we see someone kick a ball our ball-kicking mirror neurons, in our brains, fire up, even though we, ourselves, haven't actually kicked a ball or even moved our feet. The same goes for other behaviours, not so obviously physical. If others see you connecting with people, those people watching have their mirror neurons fire up. That's called empathy and for *most* people it's an automatic response. That's why 'leading by example' and 'leading from the front' are so important in most areas. It's not that people see leaders and consciously think they should be doing that too. It's their brain's automatic system and that is way more powerful and influential than 'shoulds'.

Notice the other person. See them speak. Notice then react. Ask, 'What do you think?' Systematically and persistently notice individuals. This won't happen by accident, you'll need to plan it into your schedule. Get other people to discuss who else they've connected with. Eat together.

Expertise comes from practice and feedback, not innate abilities. Not just any practice though, but specific practice aimed at improving the *memory* of the performance. A big library of cognitive maps in our brains enable experts to recognise patterns quickly that newbies cannot. Isn't that what an expert is – not someone with lots of experience and education but someone who can recognise, recall and apply patterns quickly and effectively? That's true of lawyers, plumbers, surgeons and salespeople dealing with a customer with an issue.

I've met a lot of people with lots of education and experience who are considered experts by themselves and many others. They may well be but several things can hold people back from true expertise as they gain more and more experience. One of those things is called 'Functional Fixedness'. In 1945, Karl Duncker first used this term for when people displayed a mental block against using an object in a new way that is required to solve a problem.

Over the years, the stock fun activity to demonstrate Functional Fixedness to groups in workshops is to give them a box of thumbtacks and a candle with a problem – attach the candle to the wall in a way that minimises wax drippage. In classic problem-solving, people argue and get stuck in a self-imposed set of blinkers until eventually they work out that the box the thumbtacks came in serves a purpose other than as a mere container. (Think about it.)

Another potential problem for people building experience through practice is that, as things become more familiar, our brains tend to notice *less* not *more*. We come to see things not as they are but as we assume they ought to be. Noted Russian musician Boris Goldovsky, with decades of processional experience, was one day taught a valuable lesson by a young girl he was teaching. During a piece by Brahms, he stopped her on the first beat of the bar 42 measures from the end of the piece and instructed her to play a G sharp instead of the G natural she had mistakenly played. She stood her ground and pointed out that she had played exactly what had been on the sheet music. It turned out that there had been a printing error years ago, putting a G natural where a G sharp *should* have been. (There's that word 'should' again.)

Goldovsky and every other teacher of Brahms had supposedly read that sheet music with hundreds, if not thousands, of students over many years. They had never noticed the error despite their education and experience. In fact, it was their education and experience which *caused* them to make that error.

The best teachers consistently reinforce even moderately good performance and rapidly alternate between teaching and questioning, creating cycles of rapid feedback. Such questioning gets mirrored in the mind of the student to the point where that, even in the absence of the teacher, they question themselves and the feedback on their own performance. (Anableps anyone?) This is handy to know for leaders in the workplace as you can't be everywhere all the time.

Valuable feedback arises from learning from mistakes, but this can be stifled if the unspoken question is, 'Who is to blame?'

Stop →Think →Act

What does this idea mean for you personally?

What might this idea have to do with someone you lead?

Thinking about a particular person you lead, what is the ratio of positive to negative comments they get and how can you influence that towards the ideal?

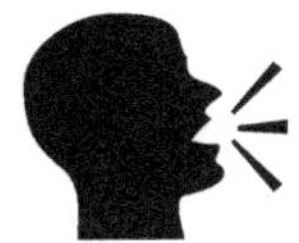

Deliberate Practice

In 1993 Swedish psychologist Anders Ericsson found that winners practise in very different ways to average people. Others have found that it's not just sports people, musicians or chess players but in areas of non-technical skills like:

- Emotionally connecting with a troubled teen.
- How to get along with co-workers.
- Talking to a superior or an expert about their error.

Malcolm Gladwell gets a lot of credit for popularising the notion that you don't become a true expert at something until you've put in 10,000 hours into that specific task. Fair enough as he's popular and tells a great story but it's Ericsson's research that came up with that finding originally. (Even noted psychologist Daniel Khaneman referenced it in his book, joking that he was the 10,000th author to quote Gladwell's 10,000 hours.) People toss that figure around without adding the important bit. It's not just the quantity of the time but the nature of the practice.

A study of software engineers showed that beyond five years' work experience, further improvements did not correlate to time spent at the job.

If you're passionate about buying shares, performing stand-up comedy or shot-putting and you've worked out that 10,000 hours is pretty much a fulltime job for ten years (less if you work weekends, which you probably would if you were truly passionate), then to get the best out of that investment of time you need to follow Ericsson's recommended 'Deliberate Practice' method:

- Full uninterrupted attention on-task for brief periods.
- Immediate feedback provided against a clear standard (testing).
- Break mastery down into mini goals (eg a daily log).
- Goals are focused on process not results (Not 'making the free throw' but 'keep my elbow in').
- Explain failures specifically ('My elbow was out' rather than 'I lost concentration').
- Regular proof of progress demanded before they're willing to admit they've learned anything or applying their new skills for real.

Ericsson's paper says Deliberate Practice:

1. Is not inherently enjoyable.
2. Is not play or paid practice.
3. Is relevant to the skill being developed.
4. Is not simply watching the skill being performed.
5. Requires effort and attention from the learner.
6. Often involves activities selected by a coach or teacher to facilitate learning.

'Deliberate Practice' is action that's overtly planned to improve performance, aims at objectives just past your level of competence, gives feedback on results and involves high levels of repetition. It is not just spending hours and hours strumming, kicking or typing.

Perseverance and resilience featured in this study as well, with Ericsson identifying consistency as the key, 'Elite performers in many diverse domains have been found to practice, on the average, roughly the same amount every day, including weekends'.

'If it's important, do it every day; if it's not important, don't do it at all.' – Dan Gable, Wrestling Coach

I once MC'd for cyclist Sarah Ulmer at a conference. She had just won a gold medal at the 2004 Olympics after having to settle for fourth place at the 2000 Olympics in the Womens' 3000m individual pursuit. She gave a powerful visual metaphor when she stressed that the difference between her fourth placing and the bronze medal she could have won was the equivalent of the radius of one of her bicycle wheels – the length of a single spoke. She held up her hands to indicate the small distance and stress her point.

That tiny distance between medal and no-medal was the one morning she slept in, or the one training session where she didn't quite put in her best effort. That realisation stuck with her for the next four years in her preparation, resulting in her gold at Athens. As Ericsson showed, but Ulmer demonstrated, consistency is the key. We need to learn when it comes to practise in the workplace where 'practice' occurs on-the-job, leaders need to create and maintain a culture where the aim isn't just to get a task done but to get better at doing it.

That mindset shift results in people:

- Processing information more deeply.
- Retaining information longer.
- Wanting more information on what they're doing.

- Seeking other perspectives.
- Adopting a longer-term point of view.

After having read Ericsson's research, I had it handed to me on a plate that, despite all my passions over the years and thousands of hours invested in activities ranging from writing to basketball to comedy to speaking to training, not much if any of that time was genuinely deliberate practice as described by Ericsson. Once they invent that time machine and I get a chance to speak with fifteen year old Terry, that's the first thing I'll tell him. I'm just off to have a chat with my kids. You carry on reading.

Stop →Think →Act

What does this idea mean for you personally?

What might this idea have to do with someone you lead?

Thinking about a particular person you lead, how can you generate more opportunities for them to get time for truly deliberate practice?

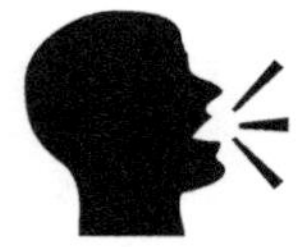

Inattention (The Invisible Gorilla)

I've been using a YouTube video of a British cycling safety advert in one of my presentations for a while now. In it, a narrator asks us to watch two groups of people. One group in white t-shirts will pass a basketball amongst themselves and move about. In amongst them a black-shirted team will do the same thing at the same time. The stated task is to count the number of times the white team passes the ball. The action ensues then stops and we are informed that the answer is 13 ... and did you notice the moonwalking bear?

The video rewinds and repeats and, sure enough, someone in a black bear costume dances into the frame, waves, and dances off. I get my audiences to follow the narrator's instructions. Aside from those who have seen it before (and that number is now well into the tens of millions), 86% of people do not see the bear that is quite plainly there to be seen. The point the video makes is that we tend to not notice that which we're not focusing on. This illusion of attention is called 'Inattentional Blindness'.

That's obviously a critical factor for cycle safety. Even well-meaning drivers looking around them constantly do not see cyclists. They're looking for others like themselves – other cars. Later we'll cover how money affects our attention as shown by Alfie Kohn's experiment where participants are given cash for remembering words on cards, but they are almost unable to remember any of the word cards' colours. That wasn't what they were focused on so their incidental learning was minimal. The same goes for our incidental attention.

How many times have you gone to look for a specific item in the fridge that always lives in the same place, like a beer, but it's not there? You declare forlornly to your housemates that you've run out, only to have someone else open the door and extract the thing you yourself couldn't find ten seconds earlier? It wasn't where it was supposed to be. It may only have been inches away but that's enough if you're narrowly focused and lacking incidental attention. You don't expect it to be *there* so you don't see it.

The moonwalking bear was originally demonstrated as an invisible gorilla by Christopher Chabris and Daniel Simons. They sometimes tweak the experiment. Asking viewers to count bounce passes and aerial passes, thus increasing the complexity of the task and the intensity of the focus required on the white team. This increased the failure rate to spot the gorilla a further 20%.

They looked at the people who did notice the gorilla. What was so different about them? One group stood out – basketballers. They had a particular expertise embedded in their brain's automatic system and so had much more precise expectations and were more open to expecting the unexpected, but only in a basketball-specific context. Hiring Michael Jordan to be your Quality Manager at work is not going to solve your problems.

It's interesting but is Inattentional Blindness a problem? Many countries have passed laws prohibiting drivers from using cellphones while driving. Studies have shown that not only do cellphones distract us, but the illusion of multi-tasking, driving and talking on the cellphone, greatly increases the odds of error thanks to our limited conscious minds. People think that they can drive and use a cellphone at the same because they have yet to have a personal experience that proves they cannot. Most times people talk and drive at the same time, nothing bad happens regardless of their split attention. They were lucky. And the drivers who do make mistakes due to their being distracted don't notice. How could they? They were distracted.

This works two ways. Not only do we miss things that are there, sometimes we subconsciously put things in that aren't there. Chabris and Simons conducted a study where participants were given a list of words to recall:

> Bed, rest, awake, tired, dream, wake, snooze,
> blanket, doze, slumber, snore, nap, peace, yawn, drowsy.

In writing up their lists of the words they remembered, 40% of participants 'remembered' seeing the word 'sleep'. It isn't there. We can assume why they think they did. All the other words are sleep-related. Like the beer in the bottom shelf of the door in the fridge, it *should* have been there.

47% of people believe memories don't change. They do. 63% believe memories are like video recordings. They're not. Our minds reconstruct memories and does so by relying on patterns. William Brewer and James Treyens did a study on people's recollections of what was in an office waiting room they'd only just been sitting in moments before. Many people recalled filing cabinets and bookshelves that weren't there.

There's change blindness and, worse still, there's change blindness blindness. 'Inattentional blindness' is not noticing the moonwalking bear. 'Change blindness blindness' is refusing to believe me when I tell you there was a moonwalking bear and insisting I replay the video three times. A study was run where participants were shown a short movie and instructed to write down the key action points as they happened. Most people did quite well. It was a short film, just two scenes, a phone call and a man walking between rooms. What nobody noticed (literally 0%) was that during the scene change the actor playing the only character in the film changed, as did his clothes. That's interesting, possibly funny and, given everything we now know about our brain's attention and focus, not surprising. But the key learning from the study was that 95% of participants believed that if that had happened, that they would have noticed. It did and they didn't. So for the aspiring Peter Jacksons and Steven Spielbergs of this world, if people are noticing the continuity errors in your film, then they're not really into your film.

Interviewed by David Hall in *The Listener*, Daniel Kahneman, for all of his years of research into psychology and heuristics and his Nobel Prize, couldn't come up with a solution to our inherent change blindness blindness. But he did have some advice, 'When the stakes are high, you should slow down'.

Some memories are sacred though, aren't they? The birth of your first child, your wedding day (well, your first one anyway), finding out your partner cheated on you, what you were doing when you heard JFK got shot. These are called 'Flashbulb Memories'. Don't trust them. But they're so vivid, so rich and detailed! They're quick to recall because of the strong emotional element to them. That's precisely why you cannot trust these memories most of all.

Psychologist Philip Tetlock studied the predictions of political scientists. Most systematically remembered their forecasts as being more accurate than they actually were – kind of a convenient 'mistake amnesia'. As he observed, it is hard to ask someone *why* they got something wrong, when they believe they got it right. Tetlock was also the researcher who found that, when it comes to predicting the future, experts were only slightly more accurate than the dart-throwing monkey I mentioned at the start of this book. Even the sharpest of experts were bested by arbitrary rules such as, 'If in doubt, assume everything stays the same'.

Daniel Simons and Daniel Levin, from Cornell University, in 1996 conducted what has been cited frequently on the internet as 'the coolest psychology experiment ever'. That's a big statement but I think you'll find it's both pretty cool, highly revealing and provocative. Search YouTube for 'Simons and Levin change blindness'.

A researcher in the role of a tourist asking for directions and carrying a map approached random pedestrians in a park. During the conversation, two other men (confederates of the researcher) walked past carrying a door. Only they didn't walk past, they walked *between* the researcher and the pedestrian while they were conversing. While briefly out of sight, the tourist switched places with one of the door carriers. That door carrier remained with the pedestrian and continued the conversation as if he were the tourist. How many pedestrians noticed the change? 46%.

Those who *did* notice were similar to the stranger. People notice people who are like them. Variations on the experiment, with the researcher dressed as a construction worker, dropped the percentage noticing the change to 33%. People's brains will categorise others into convenient categories unless there is a particular reason not to. If you want to remember someone, try judging their face for emotional traits such as honesty. The effort and the emotional connectivity make it more effective when trying to recall people. This technique gets that emotional subconscious involved. May as well make it work for you for a change!

We believe we're seeing the world perfectly well until it's drawn to our attention that we don't.

Edme Mariotte developed this next activity in 1668. Close your left eye. Focus your right eye on the +. Bring the page slowly closer to you until... *the circle vanishes.*

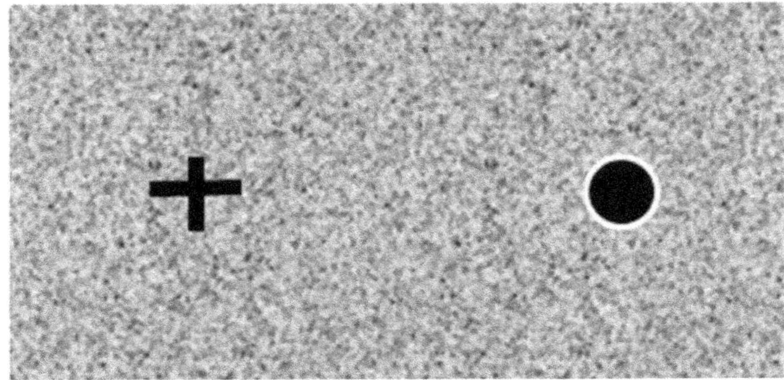

We've talked about inattentional blind spots but this is a *literal* blind spot. We've all got one. But our brain won't let us see *nothing* in that little zone so it fills it in as best it can with what it's got. Which, in this case, is more of the grey graininess of the box the circle and cross are in. The brain makes assumptions about what it sees (and remembers), not just with our literal blind spots but all the time.

Back in the mid-1990s I worked as a trainer for the New Zealand Lotteries Commission. In addition to training the franchise owners how to run the business and their staff how to sell tickets, we provided training on sales. After one session on what we called 'Retail Theatre' about how to structure sales promotions for dramatic impact and effect, one owner, Dave, was particularly fixated on one statistic I gave the group. Dave's eyes bugged out when he heard that, on average, outlets that sold a first division winning ticket could boost sales the following week by 30% simply by making their existing customers aware of that fact. Dave was a very experienced retailer. The Lotto franchise was merely a part of his larger bookstore but it was consistent and predictable, if not always a huge money spinner. 'It pays the rent,' Dave said. So, Dave knew he needed to make hay while the sun shone and winning a first division should be the sunniest week of any Lotto store's year.

My training included in-store follow-ups a few weeks later to help reinforce the transfer of learning into the workplace. So, I kept in touch with Dave and would jokingly ask him how his plans were going for when he sold that winning ticket. He seemed quietly confident that a thorough promotion would crack into action with military precision the moment the lucky sixth ball dropped out of the barrel. I admired his enthusiasm and wished him well (which I seemed to do a lot of when working with lotteries). I also questioned if the military were ever actually that precise but it was just an expression and he did seem confident.

Inevitably, I got a phone call one Saturday night. Dave's store had sold a first division winner. He'd pre-arranged with his local newspaper and radio station to run some advertisements, the templates for which he'd pre-prepared. (I realise 'pre-prepared' isn't an actual word and 'pre-arranged' probably shouldn't be. The first 'pre' is unnecessary but it does emphasise, for the story, just how much effort, planning and expense Dave had gone to). Those media outlets were given their 'go' signal the next day. I always surreally surmised that he had some CIA-style code-phrase like, 'The eagle has left the nest. I repeat, the eagle has left the nest'.

As luck would have it, in a story about lotteries, I was going into his store on the following Wednesday for our pre-arranged in-store coaching. I told him I looked forward to checking how his sales were tracking against a comparable week so we could measure the impact of his extra promotional efforts. He joked that I might have to fight my way through the crowds. He boasted most of all about his 'amazing and mind-blowing' window sign that would painted professionally early the next morning. The bulk of his promotional spend was going on the sign. I remember Dave asking, 'Tell me what you think when you see it'.

I can't remember the exact figures seventeen years later but, generally, sales of Lotto tickets increased almost exponentially throughout the week. The draw was Saturday night and almost half a week's sales occurred on the Saturday itself. I wasn't expecting miraculous numbers anytime I visited a store on a Wednesday but nevertheless it would provide a useful comparison with a week where they hadn't just sold a 'lucky' ticket. I wasn't expecting miracles but I wasn't expecting tumbleweeds either, but that is what I found when I showed up.

Dave's store was in a precinct of shops bordering a large carpark. Directly opposite the carpark was a major supermarket, the destination drawcard of the entire shopping centre. The majority of the foot traffic in the retail precinct walks out the supermarket exit which had a direct and unimpeded line of sight to Dave's main window. I drove in, parked up and walked into and out of the supermarket trying to recreate walking in the shoes of Dave's target customers. I walked to the middle of the carpark and mentally noted what I saw. Then I walked along the perimeter of the square towards Dave's store, seeing what I could see from the doorways of the other stores. I walked into Dave's store.

Once inside, the Lotto area was well merchandised, bright and clean. It was certainly uncluttered by customers. Posters were up behind the ticket terminals announcing a first division winner had been sold here. The posters were in triplicate, as they'd been trained to do so they could clearly be seen, and using an odd number draws the eye to the central message. Someone had definitely heeded our training on how critical line-of-sight was in visual merchandising.

Dave approached me with the sales reports. Sales were not up 30%. They were slightly down against the same week the previous year. What Dave seemed to find particularly galling was that he'd spent hundreds of dollars on a window sign that was not earning any return. I put my arm around him in a comforting but manly way and led him out of his store. Since the sign had been painted he had walked in and out of his own store dozens of times. I turned him around so we faced his window sign. We stood, on a sunny day, on the pavement outside his shop not three metres from the window.

'Dave, what do you see?' I asked.

'What?'

'Dave, it's a simple question. What do you see?'

'My window, what else would I see?'

I felt the need for some drama and emotion at this point because logic wasn't getting us anywhere. I stepped toward the shop window, grabbed the edge of the 1.8 metre by 1.8 metre bookcase containing bargain-basement sale books that obscured 60% of the window and tipped it to the ground. The big thud literally made an impact.

'OK, now you see your window...'

As I said, Dave was an experienced store owner. It was Dave who gave me a little quote I still use with over-confident trainees. I started out quite young and retailers tended to be a bit longer in the tooth. Some said things like, 'I've had thirty years of retail experience'. Sometimes they added the word 'sonny' at the end but even when they didn't, I always felt it was implied. One time, Dave chipped in with, 'You haven't had thirty years retail experience, you've had one year of retail experience thirty times'. Bazinga! The point I'm trying to make here is that Dave was wise and aware of the pitfalls of over-confidence.

He liked to think he walked around with his mind and his eyes open. He'd spent hundreds of dollars on a window sign, which he'd been planning for weeks and was passionate about, that could have earned him thousands of dollars. But then, at the start of each of the four business days between the winning draw and me arriving at his store he had put out that big old bookcase blocking off his own sign. This bookcase sold sale books and perhaps earned him dozens of dollars a day. Having placed the bookcase directly in front of the window sign, he then failed to notice it the dozens of times he entered in store in that four day period. Why?

The experience that Dave and most of us treasure so much has a downside. Routine and sameness are much loved and appreciated by our brains as it's less work. We've all got our routine and mindless tasks. How many of them are contributing to our own inattentional blindness?

So, it can happen to all and any of us, no matter how experienced we are, or perhaps *because* of how experienced we are. I love Chabris and Simons' closing remarks in their book about invisible gorillas, inattentional blindness and the illusions of attention, memory, confidence, knowledge, cause and potential: 'Look for the gorillas in your midst.'

Brain-Based Boss Seed Of An Idea

One supermarket I worked with had their managers do regular scheduled walk-throughs in departments that were not their own. They assessed what they saw against prescribed written criteria. Fresh eyes. Different perspectives. Plus the added benefit of managers getting exposed to new ideas in other departments.

Stop →Think →Act

What does this idea mean for you personally?

What might this idea have to do with someone you lead?

Thinking about a particular person you lead, how might you break them out of habits that might be contributing to their inattentional blindness?

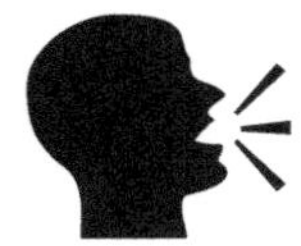

Remember What You've Forgotten

When you know something, you have a 8/5 chance of overestimating that others also know it. This is a real challenge for leaders coaching others in the workplace. You know a lot and you've forgotten what it's like to not know even the basics.

Brain-Based Boss Seed Of An Idea

One call centre I trained at made extensive use of their existing staff, from all levels and experience, during the recruitment of new reps. Senior staff took part on interview panels and frontline staff buddied potential newbies for a few hours of exposure to the reality of life on the phones. This countered, to a degree, the curse of genius, as no matter how great you were when you were on the floor/on the phones/in the field yourself, no one knows the reality of the 'now' on the coalface like those who are already there and have a vested interested in new recruits fitting in.

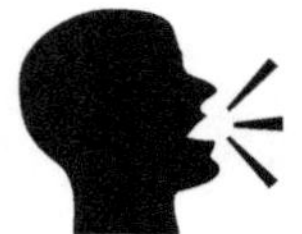

Challenge Assumptions

Psychologist Jonah Lehrer noted, 'When the brain is exposed to anything random, like a slot machine or the shape of a cloud, it automatically imposes a pattern onto the noise'. Thomas Gilovich agreed, 'Nature abhors a vacuum. People spot patterns where only the vagaries of chance are operating'. That's what pattern recognition is for, although often the brain's motto is, 'Close enough is good enough'. Chabris and Simons agree that our minds are built to detect meaning in patterns, to infer causal relationships from coincidences and to believe that earlier events cause later ones.

In his article 'Becoming Famous Overnight', Larry Jacoby wrote of his research into memory illusions caused by this cognitive convenience. Remember, cognitive processing is hard work and the brain will do anything to ease that strain. In a research study, participants were shown some names of people, including David Stenbill. Sometime later, and in a supposedly unrelated activity, they were shown another list of names and asked to tick those that were celebrities. David Stenbill, despite being fictitious and not a celebrity, was ticked more often than not. If they thought about Winston Churchill, Nelson Mandela or Margaret Thatcher, they could probably find a few facts in their memory about them and why they were celebrities. There's no genuine way they could do that for David Stenbill. All they'd have was a sense of familiarity. And for people, that's all we need. Words, and anything else we've seen before, become easier to see again.

And it's not just seeing; it's any kind of experience.

If years ago you had a conflict-ridden relationship with an employee named Toby and tomorrow you're being assigned a new employee whose name also happens to be Toby, that's not going to affect your impressions of Toby II, is it? Maybe you should give him a nickname as soon as possible?

Psychologist Robert Zajonc did a study on whether old married couples start to look like each other. This section is not about that study but it is quite interesting. It was suggested that, given the empathy couples must have shown each other over the years, much of which is conveyed through facial expressions, they develop similar wrinkle patterns. Be sure and mention this the next time you're at Gran and Pop's place.

The other Zajonc study I'm looking at here is on the mere exposure effect and links nicely with Jacoby's familiarity work. He ran newspaper advertisements on the front pages of two Michigan universities using five made-up words:

Word	Times Used
kadirga	1
saricik	2
biwonjni	5
nansoma	10
iktitaf	25

He then surveyed the student population with a simple question: Were each of these words bad or good? The words used more often were considered good more often. He replicated the study using symbols, shapes and faces and came away with the same result. Familiar was perceived as good. Familiar is safe. Zajonc suggests this may be a result of evolution as the survival prospects were poor for animals not suspicious of novelty. New things could eat you. Maybe the person resistant to change that you're leading isn't being bloody-minded? Maybe they're being safety conscious?

A downside of familiarity is the illusion of representativeness and how that bias impacts our thinking. We expect a librarian to look like our preconceived notion of one. The regression fallacy is where we sometimes choose to believe that non typical results will continue. Over time, results regress to the mean. A workplace example might be when a slightly below average performer performs especially poorly. You respond by yelling at them. Their next performance is better therefore you assume that yelling at them improved their performance. Far more likely is that their performance regressed to the mean. Golfers, you know what I'm talking about.

Stop →Think →Act

What does this idea mean for you personally?

What might this idea have to do with someone you lead?

Thinking about a particular person you lead, how might you tweak your style in dealing with them to be more effective?

Our Lazy Brains

This is another way in which our brains make their lives easier at the expense of our decision making and success. People predict the frequency of an event, or a proportion within a population, based on how easily an example can be brought to mind.

Do more people die by drowning or in fires? Many more people die by drowning, yet most people answer that question with fires. Why? Fires get attention and are emotionally memorable. They're dramatic and the media covers them, crossing over to their reporter live in the field directly in front of the vivid multi-sensory images. Any reports on drowning, if they do get reported at all, are after the fact and often told in terms of the collective statistics of the drowning toll compared to last year. That's the 'Availability Heuristic' in action. Our perception of reality is distorted by what's easily recalled.

How often have you seen someone say something only to have another member of the group respond with something like, 'That's not true. My Aunt did that every day of her life and she lived for 93 years'? They refute a fact, idea or suggestion based on a very narrow, isolated or unrepresentative example. 'Global warming, my butt. Yesterday was freezing.'

This can be annoying and unhelpful, especially if you now realise you do it all the time. But it can be turned into a useful technique as developed by Norbert Schwarz for helping the people you lead. Let's say that you lead someone you feel could be more successful if they were more assertive.

One group in the study was given two tasks:

1. List six instances in which you behaved assertively.
2. Evaluate how assertive you are.

Compared to a control group who were only asked the second question, the group felt they were significantly more assertive because they were able to list off examples. If you're dealing with someone who might be struggling in a particular area, you might want to give them the questions in advance and some thinking time rather than surprising them with a stressful and forgetfulness-inducing pop quiz. It's a fine line though. Another group's first question was tweaked to read, 'List twelve instances in which you behaved assertively'. Many couldn't think of as many as twelve. (Can you?!) This group felt less assertive than the control group. So, it's not the number of instances that mattered, it was *the ease of recall* that triggers the availability effect.

Stop →Think →Act

What does this idea mean for you personally?

What might this idea have to do with someone you lead?

Thinking about a particular person you lead, how might you tweak your style in dealing with them to be more effective?

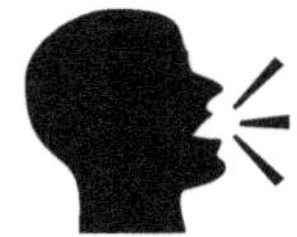

Memory

Memory is a reconstruction not a reproduction so when we're trying to recall something, it helps to be in the same state we were in when we learned it. A classic and amusing study on this involved word lists and scuba diving. In 1975, Godden and Baddeley, from the University of Stirling, compared groups instructed to memorise, and subsequently recall, lists of words. Some did their memorising in a typical classroom whereas others did so underwater. The groups were then re-split for the recalling portion of the study. Half of the landlubbers recalled on land and half under water. Half of the scuba-diving learners recalled back underwater and half in a classroom which was, hopefully, dry.

They found that what was learned under water was best recalled under water. Extensions of the study involved testing people on the content, not just recall. Again, the closer the testing environment was to the learning and recalling environment, the better the test results. Changing the environment between learning and recalling or testing reduced performance by about a third.

Stop →Think →Act

What does this idea mean for you personally?

What might this idea have to do with someone you lead?

Thinking about a particular person you lead, how can you closer connect where and how their learning occurs to how it is applied on the job?

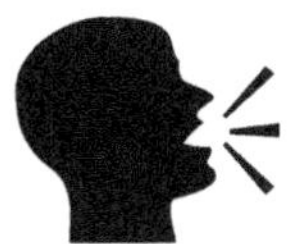

Principle 3: Autonomy

Responsibility

Bibb Latane and John Darley had a lot of time on their hands. They dropped pencils or coins over six thousand times in various situations to see if people would help them or not. If they dropped them in front of multiple people, they received help 20% of the time. If they dropped a pencil or coin in front of a single person, they got help 40% of the time.

They conducted another study where they would leak fake smoke, wafting suspiciously and dangerously, into the room where subjects of the study sat. If the subject was alone, they freaked out, on average, within five seconds. If the subject was in a group, the reaction time, on average, was 20 seconds and it wasn't a freak out as much as disinterested concern.

If you ever collapse in the street and you think you're having a heart attack, don't bother yelling to the faceless crowd for help. Use the energy you have to specially identify one individual in the crowd. 'You, the guy with glasses in the blue shorts, yes you, call an ambulance!'

You can thank me later. Better still, eat fewer pies and avoid the heart attack. Well, delay it...

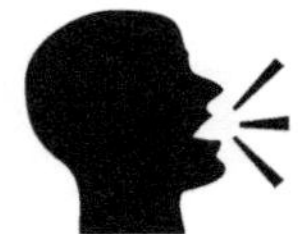

Problem Solving

'Some people cause happiness wherever they go.
Others, whenever they go.' – Oscar Wilde

As with communication, conflict resolution, and everything else we fill in a self assessment, individuals have their own particular natural style when it comes to solving problems. Styles aren't inherently right or wrong or good or bad, they are what they are. There's no 'one right way' to solve problems. And just like any other natural style we have, we can live with what we have or fight against it. This natural style is not what we are told to do or what we feel we should do. Once a person is allowed to work within their natural style, a major obstacle to peak performance is lifted.

The term 'Conation' refers to the connection of the brain's emotional processing with its cognitive processing. And as you've read, and will continue to read, getting these two systems working together as harmoniously as possible is of paramount importance for anyone's success.

You can go online and pay some cash for a quick assessment and see what your style is at www.kolbe.com. Every person has four innate strengths (some stronger than others), four modes of operating that work in combination. Have a think about your own approach to problem-solving as you read the table below:

Mode	**Description**
Fact Finder	The level of detail when gathering information
Follow Through	The method of organising information
Quick Start	The amount of risk a person takes when dealing with unknowns
Implementer	The way of handling physical and mechanical tasks

As Kathy Kolbe says, relationships suffer when we jump to the conclusion that people who act differently are trying to be difficult. Instead of trying to change each other, we would all benefit from nurturing the best each of us has to offer. Few of us would thrive under any one standard operating system or single path to success. You don't have to be one of those parents, students, patients or employees desperate to change who you innately are in a vain quest for self improvement.

This is different from Dweck's fixed mindset model, which leads people to underachieve. Kolbe isn't saying that we are what we are and we'll never change. She's talking about our personal operating systems, how we go about solving problems. Her book is called *Powered By Instinct: 5 rules for trusting your guts.* Given all we've covered so far about the elephant that is our brain's automatic system, that sounds like a good idea if we can give our elephant's rider a few guidelines.

Kolbe's research shows that of high-absentee employees 62.5% are experiencing 'conative tension'. Basically there's a misfit or intolerance between the way they're expected to do things and solve problems and the way they naturally do so.

Here are Kolbe's 5 rules:

1. Act *before* you think.
2. Self provoke.
3. Commit but to very little (Focus/Flow).
4. Be obstinate in overcoming obstacles (Grit).
5. Do nothing when nothing works.

You're nothing special if you're not yourself.

Stop →Think →Act

What does this idea mean for you personally?

What might this idea have to do with someone you lead?

Thinking about a particular person you lead, how might expectations of how they're supposed to operate conflict with their natural style?

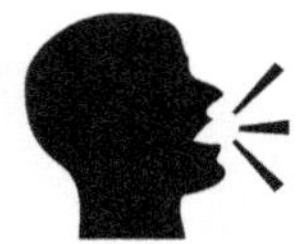

First Impressions

The Halo Effect is a cognitive bias where one trait influences our general perception of other traits of that person or object. Remember, right at the start of the book, I mentioned that interesting-but-useless study showing that people with asymmetrical faces make better leaders? Here's where the Halo Effect often kicks in, as the first thing we experience of a person is usually how they look. If we're not conscious and careful then that can unduly influence how we see everything else about them.

Solomon Asch studied this Halo Effect or, as psychologists tag it, 'exaggerated emotional coherence'.

There are two names below with a few describing words for each. Which person do you view more favourably?

Alan:	intelligent, industrious, impulsive, critical, stubborn, envious
Ben:	envious, stubborn, critical, impulsive, industrious, intelligent

Most people prefer Alan but, soon enough, you realise Ben has the same describing words but in the reverse order. Because Alan's positive words came first, they've coloured most people's perception of him positively overall.

It may be when you read Alan and Ben's descriptors that you summarised the situation clearly and logically in an instant and declared they were effectively of the same calibre. Well, this is a book full of psychological tricks and if you went into that little exercise expecting a psychological trick then that is exactly what you got. However, at work and in life you aren't waiting for psychological tricks around every corner. When you enter a job interview, meet a salesperson or conduct a performance review, you need to be aware of the potential for the Halo Effect and its flipside, which I'm choosing to call the pitchfork effect. Falling for it isn't a weakness, it's natural, if you let your brain take that easy effortless road it desires so much.

The Halo/Pitchfork Effects combine dangerously with cognitive dissonance. Daniel Kahneman not only studies and practises psychology, he also teaches it and so is compelled to mark exams and term papers. Often they come in bunches and often there are multiple pieces of work from the same students. He found that the first piece of work he marked for each individual influenced his subsequent marking for that same individual. For example, if I scored highly on the first paper, that must mean I'm good at psychology. That subconscious assumption gets me the benefit of the doubt every time Kahneman subsequently marks my work. Yet it also works to my detriment if the first piece of work scored poorly. Ambiguity gets forced to fit an existing pattern. Kahneman attempted to allow for these effects by insisting the papers arrive as anonymously and randomised as possible.

If you're leading someone and they make a mistake, to what extent is your reaction to that mistake coloured by your initial experiences with that person? This is called the 'Diagnosis Bias'. Once we label someone, we put on blinders to any evidence that contradicts the label.

Homophily is the tendency to like people who are like us. How often, when conducting a job interview, your 'good feeling' about a candidate is due to homophily?

I have to add one last comment about Kahneman as I've referenced him a lot. He's a psychologist, yet his co-development of the theory of behavioural economics he won a Nobel Prize – in *economics*. That's not even his main discipline. How does that go down at academic parties? 'Oh, you got a Nobel Prize? I got one too, for economics, AND I'M NOT EVEN AN ECONOMIST!' (I did look up the Nobel website. They don't call it 'Economics'. They call it 'The Economic Sciences'. Who says the Swedish don't have a sense of humour?)

Stop →Think →Act

What does this idea mean for you personally?

What might this idea have to do with someone you lead?

Thinking about a particular person you lead, how have you labelled them based on early impressions? What evidence is there to contradict that impression?

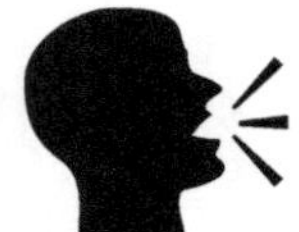

Ego

This research reveals that people overestimate the extent to which their actions and appearance are noted by others. Thomas Gilovich, from Cornel University, clearly had a sense of humour as well as a thirst for psychological discovery. Participants (who all happened to be university students) were required to wear a t-shirt that was proudly emblazoned with a large headshot of Barry Manilow, and then briefly visit a room with other people in it. Presumably Barry was chosen because contemporary students might consider him to be embarrassingly uncool. (Do kids still say 'uncool'?) Once back outside the room, the participant was asked how many of the people noticed what was on his shirt. The result was about half. The true proportion of people who did notice Mister Manilow was about 20%. And, bear in mind, if it was something less jarring than Barry, that figure would have been even lower.

People presume that other people notice them way more than they actually do. We are not the centre of the universe.

Stop →Think →Act

What does this idea mean for you personally?

What might this idea have to do with someone you lead?

Thinking about a particular person you lead, to what extent is their sensitivity to others' opinions of them affecting their performance and how might you influence this?

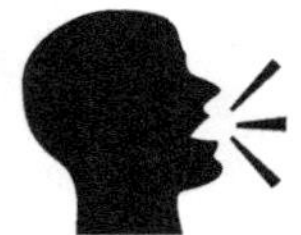

The Dangers Of Cash Incentives

Have you ever been talked into helping out a friend? Maybe they were shifting house or they needed a ride to the airport? If you accepted the request, why did you? What was in it for you? How different is that from being asked to do something at work that's a bit above and beyond the call of duty?

A group in the U.S. promoting services for their membership of retired persons asked local lawyers if they'd consider doing legal work for their members at a massively discounted rate of $30 an hour. Very few said that they would. Then they asked lawyers if they'd consider doing legal work for their members for free. Most said that they would. What!?

Voluntarily contributing some pro bono hours for a group of people like your own granny is relative to social norms. It is the sort of thing that most people would do. If you reframe that against market norms by introducing the token payment, working for cheap is not what most people would do. I know myself, as a comedian, when performing for charity fundraisers when I'm technically donating my time and services, I always still invoice the 'client'. The invoice notes the full amount of the true value of my work but also includes a 100% discount. My brand's perceived worth doesn't get devalued in the marketplace and they get a show of high value at no cost to them.

Dan Ariely ran a study where subjects were asked to perform a repetitious task on a PC for five minutes dragging circles onto squares and keeping score of how many were successfully dragged. Some subjects were paid $5 for their five minutes. Some subjects were paid 50 cents for their five minutes. The third group were simply asked to do it as a favour.

Group	Avg Score
Paid $5.00	159
Paid $0.50	101
Favour	168

OK, so people might work for a decent wage but they won't for a token cash payment but they'll bust their hump when it's a favour. What if it's not cash but a gift of equivalent value?

Group	Avg Score	2nd Study	Avg Score
Paid $5.00	159	Fancy Chocs	169
Paid $0.50	101	Snickers Bar	162
Favour	168	Favour	168

So, gifts have a greater influence on performance than their cash equivalent, almost the same as a favour. What Ariely strongly suggests is to not tell the receiver of the gift the cost of the gift. That kills the effect and reverts it back to framing against market norms. Snickers may be packed choc-full o' nuts but only monkeys work for peanuts. And it might be classy to buy a lady two twenty-dollar glasses of wine at a bar but if you offer that same lady $40, you're creepy.

People will over-perform for genuine social exchanges but the moment it becomes a mere transaction, people will perform to the letter of that transaction. And nothing makes an exchange transaction quicker than money. Later on, we'll talk about what you can do as a leader in your workplace to create an environment and a culture with more socially normed exchanges and less market normed transactions.

Stop →Think →Act

What does this idea mean for you personally?

What might this idea have to do with someone you lead?

Thinking about a particular person you lead, how might you tweak your style in dealing with them to be more effective?

Reciprocity

Psychologist Robert Cialdini conducted a cute little study involving those colourful and ubiquitous Post-It notes. He gave the appearance of conducting a simple postal survey where subjects were sent a covering letter and a survey to complete and return. There were four variations:

Variation	**Response**
Just a typed covering letter	36%
Covering letter with a handwritten comment	48%
Covering letter with a handwritten comment on a Post-It note	75%
Covering letter with a blank Post-It note	42%

Why was the return rate more significant for the handwritten comment on a Post-It note? One reason was reciprocity – the basic human need to return positive actions with positive actions. The extra effort of the sender they perceive from the Post-It note influences them to make the extra effort to respond.

Dennis Regan's 1971 study is often cited when it comes to reciprocity. At a staged art gathering, he mingled with other guests. At various times, he'd say he was going to buy himself a coke. Sometimes he would come back with two cokes and gift one to the other guest. Sometimes he wouldn't. At the end of the art show, he would then ask guests to buy some raffle tickets so he could win a prize for selling the most tickets. The coke recipients bought way more raffle tickets, often exceeding the value of the gifted coke. It was due to reciprocity. Even people who never wanted the coke, or didn't even like coke, bought raffle tickets. It's a fundamental human social driver. (Reciprocity, not coke.)

How do people apply this in workplaces? Waiting staff looking for tips are a great source of measurable results. David Strohmetz conducted a study on tipping and the age-old tradition of offering up a lolly with the bill. Compared to offering zero lollies, one sweet resulted in a 3% increase in average tips. Gifting two sweets got a 14% increase. The best result came via a slight twist in technique. Offering at first a single piece lolly but then adding an extra 'bonus' lolly like it was a last-minute secret-squirrel favour, scored a 23% increase.

Reciprocity is easy and effective but also potentially highly manipulative. Used shallowly and manipulatively in an employment context it's easy to see through quite quickly. Nevertheless it's a useful tool if used ethically and sensibly. At the very least, you need to be aware of it in case someone is using it on you...

Stop →Think →Act

What does this idea mean for you personally?

What might this idea have to do with someone you lead?

Thinking about a particular person you lead, how might you ethically leverage reciprocity in dealing with them to be more effective?

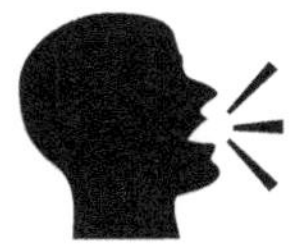

Influence Triggers

Russell H Granger identified seven internal influence triggers. As you get to know the people you lead, and the situations in which they find themselves, you'll get to know which triggers apply to them. As we work through the triggers, have a think about yourself in a situation where you've been sold something by a really effective salesperson.

1. Friendship (commonalities, sameness).
2. Authority (not hierarchical status but expertise and credibility).
3. Consistency (connecting to emotional memory as laugh tracks do with TV sitcoms. Try finding out how your person has acted in the past in similar situations).
4. Reciprocity.
5. Contrast (comparing to less favourable alternatives).
6. A Reason Why.
7. Hope.

As Granger notes, these are not logical triggers, they're emotional and seated in the brain's amygdala. Rather than fighting nature and getting frustrated, as you insist on appealing to people using rationalisation, try working with the predictable emotional responses. Appealing to logic is ultimately... illogical.

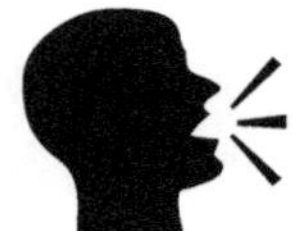

Caring

Paul Slovic at the University of Oregon researched charitable giving. In one study, he ran two parallel approaches in requesting donations on behalf of *Save The Children*. One approach gave statistics on the millions of starving children. The other was simply accompanied by a photo of a single starving child.

Approach	**Resulting Average Donation**
Stats on millions of children	$1.25
Photo of one child	$2.50

The presence of individuals affects our thinking and decision making more than we realise or, perhaps, wish to admit. Stanley Milgram conducted an infamous experiment in 1961 where students were convinced by authoritative men in white lab coats to give fatal doses of electric shocks to other students. I'd probably better elaborate. No students were harmed in the making of this experiment. A volunteer would show up, meet someone who was supposed to be another volunteer, but who was actually in on the whole thing, and engage in a fixed lottery to see who would be the 'teacher' and who would be the 'learner'. The real subject would always become the 'teacher' while the learner would be strapped into a chair and have electrodes attached to them. The teacher and the researcher then went to a neighbouring room with no view of the plugged-in learner. The teacher was then instructed to test the learner with a series of questions and for each wrong answer they would give the learner increasing levels of electric shock. They did so to fatal levels 65% of the time, despite hearing a pre-taped audio of protests, screams, pleading, claims of heart trouble and eventual silence from next door.

The one variable that affected how people behaved more than any other was the simple presence of another person. If that one person advocated upping the voltage the 65% became 90%. If that one person didn't advocate upping the voltage, the 65% became 10%.

It's not so much the power of one as it is the power of the right one.

Stop →Think →Act

What does this idea mean for you personally?

What might this idea have to do with someone you lead?

Thinking about a particular person you lead, who is their primary influencer at work and how can that relationship be leveraged?

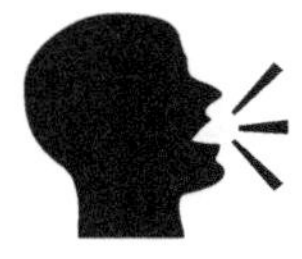

'The Way Things Are Done Around Here'

In the late fifties and early sixties, psychologist Harry Harlow at the University of Wisconsin–Madison conducted a series of experiments with rhesus monkeys that would, today, be considered very cruel. One of those studies involved bananas, a step ladder and unwritten rules. Most of the jobs I've had have involved usually two of those three things at any given time.

Five monkeys in an enclosure were gifted a step ladder and from the ceiling Harlow suspended a banana from a rope just high enough that it could be seen by the monkeys but not reached without the aid of the step ladder. Soon enough, the sharpest monkey ascended the ladder. The moment it did so, all the monkeys were blasted with freezing water from a high-pressure hose. (This, by the way, was not even close to being the cruellest experiment he conducted.)

If, at any stage, any monkey ascended the ladder, once again, every monkey got waterblasted. Quickly, the group's behaviour established a pattern. If any individual monkey looked like they were going to ascend the ladder, the other monkeys beat him into submission.

They replaced one of the five monkeys with a new monkey who had not been party to, nor had witnessed, the water blasting. The newbie saw the banana and did the logical thing – ascend the ladder – or at least it tried to before it was beaten by the other monkeys. Gradually the original monkeys were, one at a time, replaced by new monkeys oblivious to the unwritten rules of the group or the original negative reinforcement of the water blasting. Each of these new monkeys participated in the beatings and none ever again attempted to ascend the ladder. *This continued even when there were no original monkeys left.*

Cruelty aside, and before you dismiss the relevance of this to us humans, how many times have you experienced unwritten rules, or even written ones, where the people involved have no idea why things are done this way but do it anyway?

I worked my way through university at a building supply warehouse. I got the job via a student job search subsidy. I wasn't aware of it at the time but the other storeman had been highly opposed to working with 'some bloody snooping student'. I started to a chilly reception and job one on day one was to clear out the top level on a storage rack that hadn't been looked at in a long time. I can't say for certain but I'm quietly confident asbestos was the least of my problems.

Being young and stupid (though I'm not young anymore), I finished with a few minutes left in the day and went in search of the guys to see if there was anything else I could do to help. I found them loading sheets from out the back onto a small pick-up truck. The moment I walked into the back storeroom they stopped what they were doing the way everyone in the saloon in a cowboy movie always stops when the new guy in town walks in. They stared. I couldn't quite work out why. I jumped up on the truck and helped them load. They carried on.

The next day I received a much warmer welcome and a much less crappy set of tasks. Some years later I worked out why. I had walked in on them stealing and unknowingly helped them to do so, thus gaining acceptance to the group. As it turned out, they weren't really stealing. What they were taking were packing sheets. These were the top and bottom sheets from packs of wall-board often damaged and used as protection for the good sheets from the tight strapping. To the untrained eye, they looked fine but weren't really saleable. It was just the way things were done. The storemen went through the pretence of 'stealing' the sheets, even though management didn't want the sheets. Their view was that they were removing the trash.

All this was known by the original storemen but not by the current crew who did the things they did because that was the way things were done around here.

We also sold stepladders. But not bananas.

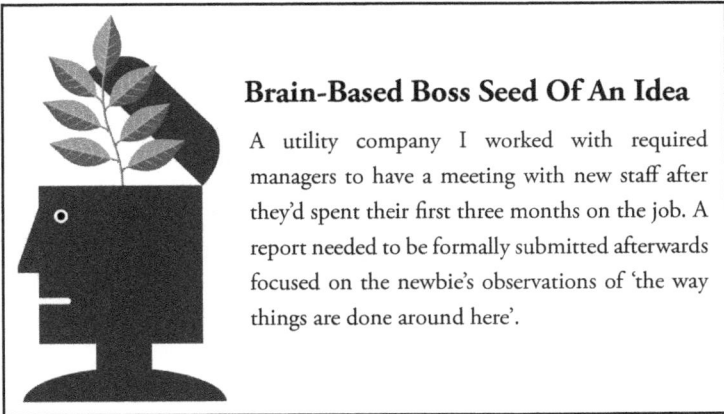

Brain-Based Boss Seed Of An Idea

A utility company I worked with required managers to have a meeting with new staff after they'd spent their first three months on the job. A report needed to be formally submitted afterwards focused on the newbie's observations of 'the way things are done around here'.

Stop →Think →Act

What does this idea mean for you personally?

What might this idea have to do with someone you lead?

Thinking about a particular person you lead, how might you tweak your style in dealing with them to be more effective?

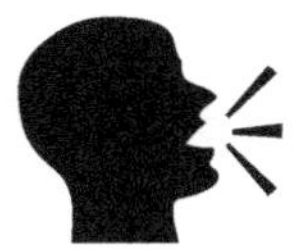

Physical Environment

Law Professor Cass Sunstein and economist Richard Thaler coined the term 'Choice Architecture' in their book *Nudge*. It describes how decisions are influenced by how the choices are presented. While they didn't literally mean architecture in the sense of plans for a building, sometimes the physical layout of a location can strongly influence the decisions that are made there. Look around your workplace. Check out the next store you walk past. There is no neutral architecture. Even doing nothing intentionally influences the behaviour of others.

Research conducted in some American school cafeterias has showed that the location of the food on offer can impact consumption of food type by 25%. If those fatty snack foods aren't right in our faces, we do tend to buy less of them. How's your willpower when passing those end-of-aisle 'specials' displays at your supermarket? Never shop when you're hungry!

My favourite example of influencing behaviour through simple environmental design is Aad Kieboom's urinal fly. Kieboom was an economist yet in the 1990s was put in charge of directing the building expansion of Amsterdam's Schiphol Airport. I'm sure they did a lot of other marvellous things during their renovations but what really got the internet buzzing was their urinal fly.

Without getting into too much graphic detail, men are grossly inaccurate in bathrooms and there are costs associated with that – cleaning is one and psychological scarring is possibly another. By simply embedding the image of a fly on the porcelain of the urinals, they reduced spillage by 80% (please do not seek out the individual researchers who measured that. I think they'd rather move on). Maybe it's the novelty factor? Maybe it's a damning indictment of the male psyche? (They tried a simple black dot instead of a fly. It didn't work.)

They wanted a behaviour change. Asking nicely and appealing to sensibilities and reason had failed. A cheap and simple bit of choice architecture drove a major behaviour change. Neat.

And if you don't think it's neat, think again the next time you push a door that's supposed to be pulled then look up to see a sign that says *PULL* in bold impossible-to-miss print. There's a classic Gary Larson *Farside* cartoon where this occurs. Unmissable, next to the door is a sign that says, 'Midvale School For The Gifted'.

Signs are a typical tickbox solution. Someone thinks to themselves that they need to communicate something. They put up a sign. They tick a box and feel that communication has occurred. Nope. I'm sure the airport toilet people, society in general and mums everywhere have communicated strongly that men shouldn't urinate on the floor. But it was Design that achieved effective communication. The message's meaning was received, understood and *acted upon*! How difficult is it to anticipate the door push/pull embarrassment occurring by designing a door that intuitively looks like it needs to be pushed or pulled? Put a sign up as well if it makes you feel better.

People often drive off from petrol stations without their car's petrol cap. People walk away from ATMs without their card. These are called 'Post-Completion Errors'. They are entirely predictable and can be prevented or mitigated through physical design and choice architecture. What such errors happen in your workplace and how might a minor tweak to the physical environment positively affect behaviour?

Some hospitals have their computer background images of bacteria. It's not bacteria clipart either. It's images of bacteria taken from doctors at their own hospital who had failed to wash their hands correctly. Back in the 1960s, Emery Freight pioneered the use of uniform shipping containers, yet checks initially showed that their containers were properly filled only 45% of the time. In shipping, time and container space is money. They came up with a solution that improved the 45% figure to 95%. They painted a line on the walls of the container with the words, 'Fill to here'. Remember Thomas Gilovich said, 'One of the most important findings from my field of psychology is that the tiniest little change in circumstance can have big impacts on people's behaviour'.

We've covered individual behaviour being impacted by changes to the physical environment. What about group behaviour? Specifically, what about group *interaction*? You've already read how positive comment ratios, social interaction and frequent feedback stimulates internal motivation and productive group dynamics. Studies show that the number one factor in influencing those who collaborate effectively at work is *physical proximity*. This might be the single most obvious finding I came across in my research. We tend to work with, and hang with, those who are already around us. Frequent exposure to these people at our desk, over coffee or in the hallway over time generates 'propinquity' – an attraction born of familiarity. (There's that word again.) How does the physical set-up of your work encourage those that need to collaborate to do so?

Stop →Think →Act

What does this idea mean for you personally?

What might this idea have to do with someone you lead?

Thinking about a particular person you lead, how is the physical layout of the workplace and the path of their movements affecting their dealings with others?

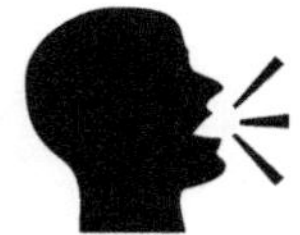

Decisions

Have you been out to a restaurant with friends recently? What did you order? What did everyone else order? Did their order affect your decision?

Dan Ariely ran some structured observations on diners. Some groups were asked to make their choices privately by ticking paper menus. Others did the more traditional approach with waiting staff asking, 'May I take your order?' The private approach produced a much wider variety of choices. The out loud and public approach produced a lesser variety of choices. Tellingly, the private orderers were significantly happier with their choices. So, it seems, many people are influenced in their choice of menu options by the decisions of their fellow diners. (Make sure you always order first!)

Psychologist Daniel Goleman, author of the book *Emotional Intelligence*, said, 'The fundamental task of leaders is to prime good feelings in those they lead'. I can just see that sending shudders down the spines of the old-school command-and-control, carrot-and-stick managers. One piece of research I found said that the average person has 12,367 thoughts a day. (A remarkably specific number, I thought.) Of these, 70% were deemed as negative thoughts. How aware are you of what you're thinking and what proportion of it is negative? If people need to hear from outside their heads a ratio of positive to negative comments of +3:1, what impact does it have on us if the voices inside our heads are commenting at a ratio of –7:3? Goleman's five domains of emotional intelligence are self awareness, self regulation (Remember Mischel's marshmallows?), motivation, empathy and social skills. Self awareness is a good place to start.

Stop →Think →Act

What does this idea mean for you personally?

What might this idea have to do with someone you lead?

Thinking about a particular person you lead, how might you tweak your style in dealing with them when they're with others to be more effective?

Principle 4: Purpose

Connection to Their Future Self

Thomas Gilovich found that of all people's regrets, 75% were regrets about *not* doing something.

Daniel Bartels, from the Columbia Business School, and Oleg Urminsky, from the University of Chicago, researched how people's sense of connection to their future selves impacted their spending and saving decisions. In their first study, students were primed by reading one of two passages about their future graduation. The first passage described graduation as a minor life event and the second passage described it as a major life event. They were then offered a choice of gift vouchers for taking part – a $120 voucher right now or a $240 voucher that would be sent some months later. Those who perceived graduation as a big deal tended to take the $120 now. People who think graduation is, in itself, a major life event are like the characters in the Bruce Springsteen song *Glory days* – doomed to live in the past. Those who see it as just one step towards more and bigger things are connected to their future selves and so went with the $240 option. What is graduation compared to first jobs, degrees, your first child, buying a house etc?

Bartels observed, 'Our work suggests that you can motivate people to hold onto their money, or make other, more prudent decisions by increasing their sense of connectedness to their future selves. Rather than trying to guilt ourselves into making prudent financial choices or creating complicated incentive schemes, we can instead look for simple, straightforward ways to foster our sense that what matters most will be preserved in our future selves, so that we can achieve goals that are important.'

A subsequent study interviewed a group of students with a simple question, 'How similar and connected are you today to the person you'll be in the future?' The results fell broadly into two categories – those who felt they were strongly connected to their future selves and those who weren't. Again they were offered a choice between two vouchers for taking part – a smaller valued one right now or a larger valued one they had to wait for. Again, those with strong connections to their future selves were far more willing to wait for the greater gain.

When it comes to long-term achievement, link into people's views of <u>WHO</u> they want to be but you'll be fighting their own low levels of impulse control. Kahneman and Tversky showed that people discount the future. Given a choice of $100 now or $110 next week, most people say they'll take the $100. Given a choice of $100 in 52 weeks or $110 in 53 weeks, most people say they'll take the $110. People will sell their future soul to the devil for a rock 'n' roll present.

That said, while people may treat their future selves like strangers, they are strongly influenced by what they perceive to be their current self image. If they, or you, can positively change that, then that can help their connection with their future self. In 1980, Steve Sharman conducted a study where people were asked by telephone to show up the next day and do three hours work for a cancer fundraiser. Half the participants were asked, 'Will you do it?' Of those that said, 'Yes,' only 4% actually showed up the next day. The other half were asked, 'Would you show up if asked?' Almost all who said, 'Yes,' showed up. People conform their behaviour to match the sort of person they think they are.

Hal Ersner-Hershfield from Northwestern University conducted a study with Stanford in 2010 on 'High Future Self Continuity'. They developed a mirror that gave subjects an avatar reflection of themselves as they would look when they were seventy years old. Compared to a control group, those having a conversation with their seventy-year-old selves set aside twice as much for retirement savings. The sooner they develop a smart phone app for that, the better.

Stop →Think →Act

What does this idea mean for you personally?

What might this idea have to do with someone you lead?

Thinking about a particular person you lead, how might you attempt to guide them into a greater connection with their future selves?

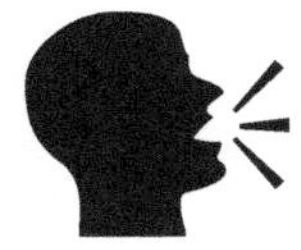

We Over-value What We Already Have

Duke University's basketball team does consistently well and its small gym is always sold out. They have a bizarre but traditional system for fairly rationing out the precious and scarce resource that is Tar Heel tickets. People have to camp out and remain present in their camps, as demonstrated in roll calls, just to get into a lottery for the right to buy a ticket. Dan Ariely got a list of those who'd made it into the draw, which showed those who'd won and those who hadn't. He rang them up and posed as a scalper offering to set up a deal for the losers to buy a ticket and the winners to sell. Bear in mind that both groups were very similar and both had gone through the highly committed, emotional and harrowing experience of the camp-out and the lottery. The average buyer was willing to pay $170. The average seller wouldn't accept less than $2400. Yes you read that right - $2400. These people were students and so $170 was a lot of money. The potential buyers spoke of it as being the equivalent of an evening out with friends plus drinks. The potential sellers justified their price by describing it as priceless, irreplaceable memories and stories for the grandkids. This seriously distorted their perception of the true value of the tickets. Be it our family home, car, job, boss or favourite TV show, we over-value what we currently have.

It is much easier to not give somebody something in the first place than to take it away from them later.

People toss around the terms ‘ownership’ and ‘buy-in’ in workplaces a lot but what do they actually mean when it comes to performance and behaviour? The more work you put into something or the greater the time, emotion and commitment invested, the greater the depth and sense of ownership. Think of the online auction bidding process, the amount of DIY projects you’ve done on your home, or trial periods for services you’ve subsequently purchased. The greater effort you’ve put in, the less likely you are to let go and walk away.

Stop →Think →Act

What does this idea mean for you personally?

What might this idea have to do with someone you lead?

Thinking about a particular person you lead, how might you tweak your style in dealing with them to be more effective?

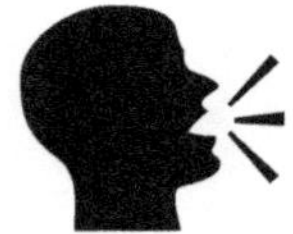

Rewards

A 1978 study by Lepper, Greene and Nisbett involved school children and their drawings. The study started with all the kids drawing, seemingly enjoying it. They were then divided into three groups and asked to continue drawing. One group was promised a reward for their drawings, one group received no promise but got a reward anyway after they were done, and the third group got no promise and no reward. All three groups were then left to continue drawing if they wanted to. Many of the children who'd been promised a reward before their earlier drawing decided not to do it anymore. The other two groups kept on drawing. What happened? The previously fun activity of drawing had been turned into 'work' by the application of *contingent rewards.* ('If/Then' rewards – as in, '**If** you do this **then** you'll get that.') And who wants to do work if you don't have to or aren't getting paid?

Sam Glucksberg conducted a study where participants were set some puzzles to complete against the clock in return for contingent rewards. One third were offered nothing for succeeding, another third was offered $5 and the remaining third $20. The $20 'high reward' group took, on average, 3.5 minutes longer than the others. Did the higher contingent reward negatively affect people's creativity and problem solving abilities?

The town of Gothenburg, Sweden had 52% of their population donating blood. They then offered a fifty Kroner reward for donating blood. The participation rate dropped to 30%. Then they eliminated the if-then reward and, instead, offered the same fifty Kroner amount as a donation to a charity in the name of the blood donor. The participation rate increased to 53%. This isn't about work versus play anymore but something else affecting people's behaviour and motivation.

When Switzerland was exploring what to do with the waste from its nuclear power generating programme in 1993, the Government found that asking people if locating the waste near their town was OK with them 'for the good of the nation', they got a 50.8% yes result in surveys. The same question, with an added offer of 5000 francs, got a yes result of 24.6%.

Brain scanning shows that the pleasure centre of the brain (nucleus accumbus) and the altruism centre of the brain (posterior superior temporal sulcus) cannot activate concurrently. You can do something for national pride or you can do something for the jollies that cash can buy you, but it seems you can't do both at the same time.

In 2000, Uri Gneezy and Aldo Rustichini looked at behaviour of parents at a childcare centre. The centre in Haifa was open from 7:30am to 4pm. They spent four weeks observing. Often, parents were late picking up their children. A ten Sheckel fine was introduced with the idea that this would encourage parents to pick up their kids on time. Late pick-ups not only increased, they doubled! Parents no longer felt guilty about being slightly late, and the sense of obligation to try and make it on time had gone, leaving a transaction where more time was being 'bought'. This perception of an obligation to a community was converted into a mere transaction by a penalty (effectively, an 'anti-reward'). This is the same as what happened with the Swedish blood donors. A sense of contribution had become a mere trading of commodity for cash. Desired participation fell accordingly. And it's the same for the kids and their drawing as work becomes play.

We are *intrinsically* motivated to do things where the very task itself is its own reward – drawing as a kid, donating blood, not letting down a carer who's looking after our child. This is a critical component of 'Flow'. Whenever you're doing something in what could be your free time, because you choose to, you're *intrinsically* motivated. It's inside yourself. The opposite is *extrinsically* motivated. Where you're doing something you wouldn't choose to do because after you do it someone else gives you something such as money, status or less nagging, that's *extrinsically* motivated.

So, what?

A lot of my training and the advice I've been taught on the job over the years has been strongly influenced by the behavioural notion of carrots and sticks. Set a performance goal. Achieve that goal and earn a bonus. Classic 'if/then' rewards. Carrots and sticks can cause problems. They can extinguish intrinsic motivation. Remember the kids who used to like drawing for its own sake and then stopped once it had become 'work'? Carrots can stifle creativity. Remember the paid problem solvers were slower than the ones doing it for fun. Carrots encourage cheating, shortcuts and skinny ethics. Carrots stimulate a part of the brain called the nucleus acumens, the same part primarily associated with addiction. Carrots promote short-term thinking. Remember that Global Financial Crisis with all its quarterly bonuses driving the ultimately destructive banker behaviour? It only turned out destructive. At the time, anyone logically focused on the carrots being dangled would've been crazy not to do what they did.

Daniel Pink, in his book *Drive: The Surprising Truth About What Motivates Us*, suggests that the traditional extrinsic reward, or 'carrot', is only really effective in a narrow set of circumstances. His primary conclusion favours intrinsic motivation and that people have a fundamental need for autonomy, contribution towards a purpose and mastery of a challenge. Doing something for a dangled reward, rather than because you choose to, fails the autonomy test.

Wouldn't it be great to have a job where you could just cruise? We've all probably thought that at times, probably during those times where the going was particularly *uncruisey*. Maybe we've even thought it would be great to just retire and potter around and have nothing to worry about.

I MC'd a health and safety conference once where Doctor David Beaumont spoke. David is an English Occupational Medicine specialist now resident in New Zealand. Part of his presentation related to case studies of people on long-term absences from work due to accident or illness. I was particularly struck by stories that described the impact the removal of responsibility and purpose had on the people and their families. It was not just, or even primarily, the *financial* ramifications, but the negative effects on their confidence, esteem and sense of self-worth, and subsequently on their *health* **and** that of their families. It also impacts on their physical recovery from the original accident. That's why getting back to even light duties is so important, not so much for the employer to minimise their costs but for the recovery of the employee. Work provides a lot more to a person than a mere pay cheque to an individual.

It reminded me of a study back in the 1970s by Ellen Langer and Judith Rodin. They had two groups of nursing home residents. Individuals in both groups were each gifted a pot plant (a legal pot plant, not an actual POT plant. That would be an entirely different study). One group was told to enjoy the plant but not to worry their pretty little heads about looking after it. All of that would be taken care of for them. The second group was given suggestions on pot plant care but the actual effort was left to the residents themselves. Because all participants were constantly being tested they were a great group to assess the impact of responsibility on health.

Within three weeks there were significant differences between the groups in health and general activity being engaged in, and it was even more pronounced after 18 months. The mortality rate of the first group (having no responsibility for their pot plants' care) was *twice* that of the group with the responsibility. In short, the quality and the quantity of many lives in that group were enhanced.

There was more to this than just pot plants but they make a nice and memorable image. The group looking after their own pot plants were also given more choice and input into the decision-making around their lives at the nursing home. I imagine this gave them a sense of control, even power to a degree. That sense of control and influence is important for all people, contributing not just to health but also happiness, success and so much more.

It isn't much of a stretch to extrapolate this thinking to the workplace. As a leader of a team, what incremental responsibilities can you arrange to boost the confidence, esteem and sense of self-worth of your people?

Although if you accidentally gift your staff a real POT plant I know a guy who can do you a great deal on workplace drug testing!

Have a think about your work place and the people you lead. Think of a particular person who you might describe as being 'unmotivated'. Think of one of their particular tasks. Is the task mostly routine? If so, can you increase the challenge or variety, make it less routine or connect it to a higher purpose? If you can, you should. If you cannot, that's the right time and place to consider 'if/then' rewards which are made more effective by explaining why the task is necessary, acknowledging the boredom and, as much as possible, letting them do it their way.

This last point is important. Even if you are resorting to extrinsic motivators, you should at least try not to stomp out what remains of their human intrinsic motivations. How can you encourage even some autonomy, mastery of a challenge, or connection to some greater purpose? Let's focus on some autonomy.

Looking at the four factors below, how can you assign people to a boring, unchallenging, repetitive task that in some small way allows them a self-perception of some control?

What people do.	(Task)
When they do it.	(Time)
How they do it.	(Technique)
With whom they do it.	(Team)

The research shows that outside of these narrow conditions, that traditional 'if/then' rewards are not only ineffective, they are counter-productive. Consider, if you must, using 'now/that' rewards. 'If/then' rewards are contingent. People are told in advance what they need to do to be rewarded and once they've done it, they are rewarded. 'Now/that' rewards can be the same reward you would've used anyway but without that pre-promised contingency. You still get to feel like Santa with company money but it doesn't extinguish people's own intrinsic motivation. As Edward L Deci implies, it's not *that* you reward, it is *how* you reward.

Think about the conditions that Pink describes as being conducive to extrinsic rewards – boring, repetitive, unchallenging, unconnected – that sounds a lot like most jobs that were created out of the industrial revolution. Bosses using basic carrots and sticks back then may literally have been using actual carrots and genuinely pointy sticks. (Good for both thwacking and poking. A blunt stick is only good for thwacking.)

My view is that people get a job and show up for money but that's about it. They'll maintain a pulse but not engage with that elusive 'discretionary effort'. Frederick Herzberg identified money not as a motivator, but as a 'hygiene factor'. Simply put, money doesn't motivate people but the absence of it demotivates.

Even when spending our own money, we are not as turned on by things as we think we are. Leaf van Boven and Thomas Gilovich found that purchases of experiences such as holidays were recalled more positively than experiences of material objects such as cars.

Somewhat controversially, author and speaker Alfie Kohn wrote a book called *Punished By Rewards* criticising businesses' and the education system's over-reliance on rewards. He lists them as, 'gold stars, incentive plans, A's, praise and other bribes'. Remember back to our chapters on how money negatively affected people's internal motivations? That's what Kohn is getting at but in greater detail. It's not that making positive statements is a bad thing. We know that it's not, thanks to Losada and his high-performing-teams study and 3:1 ratio minimum of positive to negative statements. Kohn dismisses *vague* praise in phrases like, 'Well done' when it is unconnected to any specific performance. He makes a distinction between useful positive feedback and praise as an instrument of manipulation.

In the real world, rewards must be judged on whether they lead to lasting change, change that persists when there are no longer any goodies to be gained. If rewards do work for people alienated from their work, performing tasks that are mindlessly simple, they only improve quantitative performance, not quality.

Rewards can punish, as people may fail to achieve them. Rewards can rupture relationships by creating or reinforcing hierarchies, competition, stifling teamwork and an artificial scarcity. Do rewards motivate people, he asks? Yes, they motivate people... *to get rewards.*

In one of Kohn's experiments, his participants were handed a pile of coloured word cards and asked to memorise as many as possible in a limited time. Some were offered a reward. Afterwards, as well as asking them to recall the words, they were also asked to recall each card's colour. Those offered rewards did very poorly on recalling colours. Rewards create an over-focus. They stifle 'incidental learning'. Rewards cause people to do what is specified and no more. If that's what you're after, go for it, but there aren't many jobs left like that anymore.

Sadly, Kohn talks about a programme run in some American schools to encourage reading by offering pizza to kids for checking books out of the library to read. Their rewards encouraged a specific behaviour, the checking out of books, which did indeed boom. Most of these were short books with large print. Many students who were asked basic questions about the books afterwards did poorly, but, then, that wasn't the behaviour being rewarded, was it? Worse, and sadder still, overall reading outside of school hours actually decreased, even amongst those who had been decent readers before. The pizza programme devalued reading, turning an inherently enjoyable act into work and diminished the autonomy of the students. Rewards are most dangerous when used with activities that we WANT them to WANT to do.

This reminds me of the tale of the Singapore rat bounty of the early 1920s. One measure to assist the control of their burgeoning rat population was to enlist the help of the people. A bounty per tail was offered and, subsequently, there was a big drop in rat numbers. However, a few months later, the rat population exploded. Why? People had started farming rats for the bounty...

Sergei Bubka was a Ukrainian pole vaulter of the 1980s and 1990s. Up to its collapse in 1991, he represented the Soviet Union. The Soviet government incentivised athletes for breaking new world records. Their intention was to drive performance to its highest standards but that's not what happened. Bubka became noted for setting new records by small amounts, often as little as a centimetre. He worked the system to earn multiple bonuses. Bubka broke the record 35 times. The government may have intended to incentivise the highest possible vault but what they actually incentivised was breaking the record and they got a lot of that. Which they paid for.

I have a soft spot for Kohn's thinking due to a story he tells early on in his book about how he almost failed out of psychology at the first hurdle. Conducting a study on enforced behaviour in lab rats, feeding them rice krispies every time they pushed a metal bar in their cage, he wrote his paper *from the rats' point of view*. 'Hey, I've trained a student to feed me breakfast...'

He accepts that there's certainly a bit of rat in all of us, as we've been conditioned through reinforcement throughout our lives. If you've ever taken a shower and you heard someone flush a toilet, then you leapt out of the shower stream in the expectation of avoiding the inevitable burst of overly hot water, then you know what operant conditioning is. (Hint – you're the ope**rant**.) But he refuses to accept that we should treat people like pets or that it results in long-term, meaningful behaviour change.

You'd imagine Kohn's notion of rewards as punishing wouldn't sit well with Bob Nelson, famous for books about 1001 ways to reward employees. Certainly they had a little internet spat going on for a while. I don't think they're really that far away in their thinking. In his drive to help workplaces create cultures of recognition, Nelson comes out with quotes like:

> 'You get the best effort from others not by lighting a fire beneath them but by building a fire within them.'

> 'You can't motivate others, you can only provide an environment that is more conducive to their self motivation.'

I definitely agree with the second quote. I might change the first quote to, 'You get the best effort from others not by lighting a fire beneath them but by building the fire already aflame within them'. There's a subtle but important difference. The former suggests that an external effort to provide someone with motivation which we know is doomed to fail and be continuing hard work, creating dependence. The latter is about connecting to a pre-existing, inherent and intrinsic motivation.

Gerald Graham from Witchita State University surveyed employees on what they perceived to be the most effective external motivators:

- Manager personally congratulates employees who do a good job.
- Manager writes personal notes for good performance.
- Organization uses performance as the major basis for promotion.
- Manager publicly recognizes employee for good performance.
- Manager holds morale-building meetings to celebrate successes.

I think it'd be more helpful and productive for all if we got away from the baggage of judgement-laden terms such as 'reward' and focused on creating an environment that is more conducive to their self motivation. It'd be hard to argue that Graham's five points above are a good place to start. Apart from the muffins and fruit juice (or muffin and juice equivalents) for the success celebrations, they don't cost money.

The challenge though is that many jobs, even today, are not intrinsically very motivating. As I wrote this book, I tried to keep in mind some of the incredibly diverse range of people I have trained over the years – one in particular is a lettuce stacker. I like lettuces and well stacked lettuces help me maintain my salad munching lifestyle. No one likes to take the best looking lettuce in the pile, only to experience the hell that is a public produce avalanche. Suddenly, you're getting all Neo from *The Matrix* dodging bullets and trying to catch and restack lettuces in real time.

My point is that I do value the work of a lettuce stacker and I'm not trying to diminish it. I do imagine that some people would not find that work, in itself, especially motivating. Remember 'Flow' needs the doing of the task to be the reward itself.

So, the argument goes that, given that a lot of entry-level and production jobs can be linear, unthinking and repetitious, these fancy rules of intrinsic motivation don't apply. These folks need carrots dangled.

My observations would be:

1. The trend is that there are less of these types of jobs, especially in the so-called developed nations, and they continue to decline in number.
2. Whether you find a role to be intrinsically motivating or not isn't important. What matters is how the person doing it feels.
3. The extrinsic motivators of carrots and sticks can still be in your toolbox to be worked through if necessary as a partnership. Not as a pizza-for-books manipulation, but your primary efforts should be on creating that environment conducive to employees' self motivation.

Stop →Think →Act

What does this idea mean for you personally?

What might this idea have to do with someone you lead?

Thinking about a particular person you lead with a mainly linear and repetitive role, what incremental responsibilities can you arrange to boost their confidence, esteem and sense of self-worth? How can you add autonomy through task, time, technique and team?

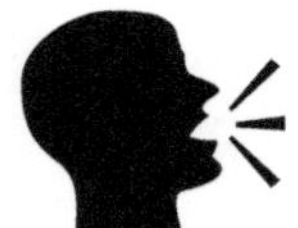

Recognition

'Credit is infinitely divisible' – Dr. Don Berwick

Research cited by Adrian Gostick and Chester Elton in their book *The Carrot Principle* says that 74% of leaders worldwide still do not practise recognition with their employees. That means 26% do. 20% would but want explicit permission from superiors. 22% reckon they could but resist. 32% believe it to be a waste of time. I'm no statistician, nor an expert on cause and effect, but these same 20% who don't believe in recognising employees have the lowest engagement levels and lowest productivity. Exit interviews showed that 79% of employees who quit stated amongst their reasons for doing so was a 'lack of appreciation'. 65% of American employees say they received zero praise or recognition in the workplace each year.

Recognition is effective because it provides a basic human need – to be seen as worthy when providing something of worth. To the survey question, 'My organisation recognises excellence,' the top scoring 25% of companies averaged 8.7% return on equity. The bottom scoring 25% of companies averaged 2.4%. (Though, in fairness, that's quite poor so maybe they didn't have any excellence to recognise?)

We can extend the impact of our recognition efforts if it's appropriate to do it publicly, get it endorsed by someone senior, repeat it or create a visible reminder.

Stop →Think →Act

What does this idea mean for you personally?

What might this idea have to do with someone you lead?

Thinking about a particular person you lead, for what should they be recognised and how would be most effective?

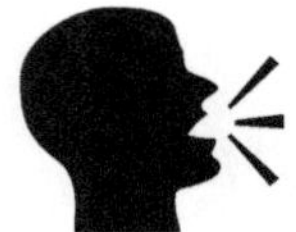

Money

Often in your life, you're doing something not because you're told to, or paid to, or because you think you should, but because you *choose* to. As a child you did this a lot, drawing pictures and building with blocks. As an adult, you've got a lot of demands on your time but in the precious discretionary time you have, you might strum a guitar, surf the sea or the internet. Chances are, you have an activity of choice that if (when) you win the lottery, you'd like to spend more time doing.

What if someone paid you to do it?

In 1969, Edward L Deci and Victor Vroom ran a study on some people playing puzzles. Half were asked to play puzzles, scoring a point for each one that was completed within eight minutes. The rest were offered $1 for each completed one. They weren't comparing the performance of the two groups in the eight minutes. They were comparing what the groups did *after* the eight minutes. Most of the paid group stopped playing when the time was up. Most of the unpaid group kept on playing because it was inherently enjoyable. Stop the pay and you stop the play. Let's remember this last phrase for later.

A survey by AMEX asked what people did with their most recent cash bonus. The top two responses were:

1. Paid bills.
2. Can't remember.

Something you need to be careful with when it comes to

money is perceptions of procedural justice and fairness. If I offered you a choice of $2 or nothing, which would you accept? Can you think of any circumstance where you would choose nothing?

In one bargaining experiment, participants, unknown to each other, were paired at random. One person out of the pair was given $10 to share with the other person. They were allowed to make one offer and if that offer was rejected, then both would get nothing. Offers of $5 each were accepted 100% of the time. Offers of $8 for the giver and $2 for the receiver were rejected more than half the time. Why? Surely, logically, $2 is better than nothing? When a supposedly random computer programme, instead of a person, made them the $2 offer, most people took it. It's about the process, not the outcome, and a perceived lack of procedural justice and fairness.

Money motivates to a degree but it undermines intrinsic motivation. It turns play into work and diverts attention from the task onto the reward. It turns players into pawns and encourages shortcuts on time, quality and ethics. The costs of trying to use money as a motivator is loss of interest, loss of excitement and vitality, and a loss of a sense of self control. I'm not knocking money. I'm a big fan of money. Money, however, is not a genuine motivational tool. What money does is... control.

Songs suggest that money can't buy you love or happiness. The research indicates that you can have a good time trying if you get the chance. Phillip Brickman studied lottery winners compared to a control group. After a brief spike post-win, the winners' happiness returned to their natural levels. The winners from that point on had about the same level of happiness as the control group but the non-winners were far happier with the simpler things in life. (Yesterday's luxuries become today's necessities.) Once the perceived 'necessity' level is achieved, money does not improve happiness.

Using brain scanning, neuro-economist William Harbaugh found that helping others activates the same parts of the brain which are activated when our basic needs are met, suggesting that helping is a basic need. How might you programme into everyone's job some aspect of helping others? It could be as a mentor, buddy or even putting in some hours towards a charitable cause.

Kathleen Vohs at the University of Minnesota studied the effect of money as a prime. She found that those primed with money-oriented stimuli will wait twice as long before asking for help. Staging a series of 'accidental' drops of a jar of pencils in an elevator when the participants left after they thought their work was done, the money-primed people helped pick up far fewer pencils. In another study, she found that two such people given a couple of chairs to sit in a room and work together sat further apart than those not primed by money. So, money does make a difference for people doing mundane tasks and will induce people to endure pain or discomfort up to three times longer. Money also helps people flog dead horses, become selfish and anti-social. Good to know.

Stop →Think →Act

What does this idea mean for you personally?

What might this idea have to do with someone you lead?

Thinking about a particular person you lead, how might you tweak your use of money in dealing with them to be more effective?

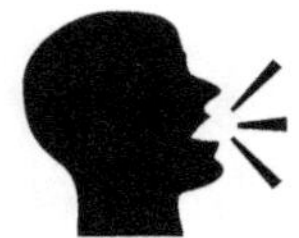

Reacting

We've already covered how realistic levels of positivity, frequent interaction and social networks can support success at work. How can you nurture these things for yourself and your team?

People do like to hear about themselves and have their decisions confirmed as wise. Rick van Baaren from the University of Nijmegan ran a study on how serving staff could influence their tips. Simply repeating customers' orders back to them and confirming their choices increased tips by 70% compared to those who didn't.

A technique that will be useful to you outside restaurants and inside your home or workplace is 'Active Constructive Responding'. Of all the techniques I ran across in my research, this is one of the best in terms of impact in return for effort. It's easy and noticeably impactful immediately, especially if you've recently had a track record of being distant, detached or a selfish jerk. Psychologist Shelly Gable of the University of California developed a framework to represent the various ways we could respond to interactions from our friends, families and co-workers.

Let's say that you've just announced to your friend that you've got a promotion at work:

Positive News	Response Type	Example
'I just got a promotion!'	Active Constructive	'Your hard work has paid off. Tell me more.'

Positive News	Response Type	Example
'I just got a promotion!'	Passive Constructive	'That's great. Are we out of beer?'
'I just got a promotion!'	Active Destructive	'That's a lot of work. Hope you're up to it.'
'I just got a promotion!'	Passive Destructive	'I had a terrible promotion experience once...'

Using the Active Constructive approach generates the greatest leverage from the good news. You're choosing to partner with your friend to capitalise on the positivity, with benefits for both of you. It's a combination of a positive statement with an enquiry, likely leading to more positive statements. Remember Losada and his minimum 3:1 ratio? This is one way of getting your average up. Remember Dweck's growth mindset for success? You need to ensure that your positive statement focuses on their behaviour not an inherent characteristic. 'Your hard work has paid off' supports a growth mindset. 'I always knew you were leadership material' supports the unhelpful fixed mindset. You should also make a deliberate open physical movement towards the person speaking, as opposed to saying the right thing while continuing to open the fridge in search of that elusive last beer.

Stop →Think →Act

What does this idea mean for you personally?

What might this idea have to do with someone you lead?

Thinking about a particular person you lead, how might you tweak your style in reacting to news from them to be more effective?

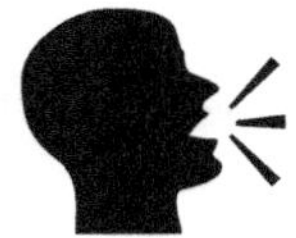

Expectations

This is probably one of the more obvious findings that I ran across. Our expectations affect how we perceive things. Taste tests have shown that people tasting a cookie from a jar with only two cookies left perceive that cookie to taste better than exactly the same cookie from a nearly full jar. Perceived scarcity affects our perception of quality. Be very wary of anything that is 'for a limited time only'.

Different people can experience exactly the same event and perceive it very differently. For example, this party is going to suck → I went to the party → the party sucked. Let's say that I think I really like Coca Cola but I think I really hate Pepsi. Give me a Coke and I'll like it. Give me a Pepsi and I'll hate it. This forty dollar bottle of olive oil in the fancy bottle that says 'Product of Spain' will be superior to the house brand six dollar bottle of olive oil.

But some people have a good time at that same party. Blind taste tests mess with the heads of both Coke and Pepsi lovers and haters. I seem to recall a former Chief Executive of Coke who was embarrassed by failing such a televised test. Plenty of blind wine tastings around the world have put the fancy and expensive 'genuine' champagnes in their places. But is it just a conscious snobbery that makes us prefer Coke/Pepsi to Pepsi/Coke or expensive products to generic substitutes? Or do our expectations influence our brains and affect the way we perceive the world? They do.

I'm not really picking on sugary fizzy drinks. Actual researchers have plugged people into MRI scanners and observed how Coke and Pepsi registers in people's brains, in both blind and labelled tests. This was quite tricky too, given that the subjects had to be horizontal and motionless. (That's how I drank quite often when I was younger.)

Sam McClure and colleagues found that in the blind tests for both drinks the ventromedial prefrontal cortex of the brain was activated. This is an emotional response centre turned on by the sugar rush. That, ladies and gentlemen, is what you pay for. But, with the Coke in the non-blind test, another part of the brain sparked up as well - the dorsolateral prefrontal cortex which connects memory, cognitive processing and emotion. Whatever their perceptions of Coke were, they were influencing the brain's unconscious responses and, in turn, their perception of the drink. This goes a long way to explaining the famous failure of 'New Coke' back in the 1980s where taste tests told them that the new recipe was much preferred by customers. And it was – in BLIND TASTE TESTS. In the reality of the stores, it died a quick death and caused a furore, now cited frequently in marketing textbooks as a model of executive failure. But it wasn't. It was a shining example of success – of the previous century of influence of brand advertising on our brains and perceptions. I said earlier that we were paying for the sugar rush. That's not true. We're paying for a combination of memory and emotional connection sparked by a red and white swirly logo.

We're not snobs. It's our brains. And in much the same way

as sugary fizzy drinks get into our teeth, years of brand advertising get into our brains.

So, if this were true, does it depend when we find out which drink is which? It should. Let's give Coke and Pepsi a break. Let's pick on beer!

Dan Ariely dressed up as a bartender at one of M.I.T.'s local pubs for a study on the timing of the effects of expectations on people's perceptions. He set up a booth at the entrance where anyone who tasted both small 'A' and 'B' samples would get a free big mug of the beer of their choice. (Both 'A' and 'B' samples were Budweiser but 'B' had two drops of balsamic vinegar added.) He ran three different tests and compared results. In the first test, the patrons were never told about the vinegar. In the second, patrons were told about the vinegar BEFORE they tasted. In the third, patrons were told about the vinegar AFTER they tasted but BEFORE they made their preference.

Oddly, those who didn't know about the vinegar mostly preferred the vinegary sample 'B'. Those told about the vinegar in advance, *almost entirely* chose the vinegar-free sample 'A'. (But, remember, they couldn't get their freebie until they'd tried both samples.) So, once again, expectations were colouring perception. But what about the group who were told about the vinegar AFTER they'd tasted? They mostly went for the vinegary sample 'B'.

One last amusing example of expectations and perceptions came out of the very unamusing Christchurch earthquakes of 2011/12. Humour is important for dealing with stress and it shone through on occasion amidst the tragic events in Christchurch. Christchurch was not at all famous for earthquakes prior to its recent big ones, but over the months and years since the first quake, the people there have endured thousands of aftershocks. People have become somewhat expert of the nuances of the Richter scale. They have a t-shirt doing the rounds: 'I don't even get out of bed for anything less than a 5.0.' Their expectations have affected their perceptions.

Stop →Think →Act

What does this idea mean for you personally?

What might this idea have to do with someone you lead?

Thinking about a particular person you lead, how might you tweak your style in dealing with them to be more effective?

Principle 5: Influence Others

You Cannot Not Influence – Priming

The very act of ringing people up to survey them on their voting intentions increases voter participation by 25%. That's an act of Priming. The simple smell of cleaning fluid can make people clean up after themselves three times as much, according to a 2005 study by Hank Aarts from Ultrecht University.

Priming is important and pervasive. Many of the other techniques rely on it to some degree. Priming also probably generates frequent accusations of being a tool of manipulation. I'll explain and address those concerns in a moment after I outline what Priming is. I will say, however, that Priming is a tool. A hammer is also a tool and used properly to bang in nails, as it designed to do, it is incredibly effective. It could also be used as a weapon or a toothbrush resulting in damage and/or ineffectiveness. That isn't the hammer's fault and doesn't justify not using or knowing how to use a hammer. This odd sidebar will become clearer soon, I promise.

An interesting example of Priming earlier in this book was when I wrote about marshmallows and Oreo cookies and you feeling hungry. It's interesting but not especially useful. Or is it?

John Bargh, Mark Chen and Lara Burrows ran a simple

study with marked results on the impact of Priming even with a simple and subtle approach. Participants were individually given sets of words to unscramble into meaningful phrases. Half were given sets loaded with words such as aggressive, rude, annoying and intrude. The other half were given sets loaded with words such as honour, considerate, polite and sensitive. All were told there was another part to the study and they needed to go to another room where an assistant would give them their instructions. On arrival, each individual found the assistant there but engaged in a conversation with another person staged to look obviously intense. How long did people take before they interrupted the conversation?

Group	**Avg Time To Interrupt**
Intrusive Primes	5.5 minutes
Polite Primes	9.3 minutes

Melissa Bateson at Newcastle University looked no further than her own workplace's cafeteria for one of their studies into influencing people's behaviour through primes. Their employer placed an honesty box for consumers of tea and coffee to put money into. I admire their optimism. Bateson and colleagues alternated their primes each week with a poster next to the honesty box. One prime poster was of flowers. Every other week, the poster was of a pair of eyes. The 'eye' weeks resulted in three times as much honesty ending up in the form of cash in the honesty box.

While not strictly Priming, I'd like to end this chapter with a couple of associated experiments on influencing behaviours.

Dan Batson of the University of Kansas ran a social experiment on fairness versus perceived fairness. Individuals were told they'd be working with a partner in another room. Each would do one of two tasks, one of which was unpleasant. You got to choose who did what and your partner would never know. (Of course, there was no partner in the other room.) The researcher left for a few minutes while the subject decided. They had a coin in a sealed plastic bag in case they wanted to 'decide fairly'. 90% of non-coin tossers gave the crappy job to their partner. Of those who said they tossed a coin, the crappy job was given to their partner 90% of the time! (Yeah, right.)

The only variable that made the decider make fairer decisions was putting a *mirror* right in front of them.

Stop →Think →Act

What does this idea mean for you personally?

What might this idea have to do with someone you lead?

Thinking about a particular person you lead, how might you tweak your style in dealing with them to be more effective?

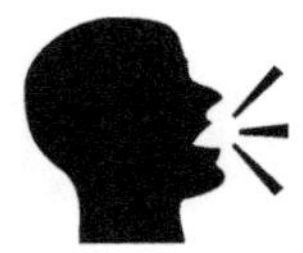

Priming and Money

Kathleen Vohs, Nicole Mead and Miranda Cook ran a study combining Priming and Market Norming to identify what particular behavioural impacts would result. Once again, good old scrambled word lists were used to prime people to think about subjects without being directly and consciously instructed to do so. (Priming doesn't work if the primee knows it is happening so you cannot easily prime yourself.) One group was primed with random word sets such as, 'The sky is blue'. The other group was primed with market-oriented word sets such as, 'High paying salary'. Everyone was then set a challenging puzzle and one of the instructions was that they could ask for help if they needed to. People were timed on how long it was before they asked for help:

Group	Avg Time To Seek Help
Random Primes	5.5 minutes
Market Primes	3.0 minutes

So, market-primed people seem quicker to give up. (No grit!) Perhaps more disturbing, findings from this team's study found that market-primed subjects were less likely to offer help to others (despite being quicker to seek it) and were also more anti-social.

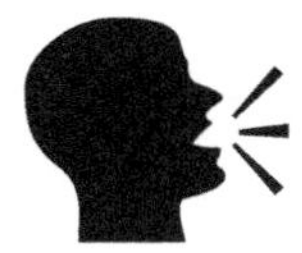

Last-Place Aversion

Ilyana Kuziemko from Princeton University and Michael Norton from the Harvard Business School wrote about a paradox they discovered after having their curiosity aroused by the 'Occupy Wall Street' protests of 2011. They thought that during a recession when 1% of the population possessed 35% of the total wealth more people would be supporting the protests. Regardless of your personal politics or ideology, you'd imagine in a recession like the one following the Global Financial Crisis of 2008 more people would start agreeing with a statement like, 'Government should reduce income differences between the rich and poor'. Actually, surveys showed that agreement with that statement plummeted during the recession, especially among poorer minorities.

They surveyed people about support for a proposed raise in the minimum wage. Those below the current minimum were supportive. No surprise there. Average wage earners were supportive despite receiving no direct benefit themselves. That's nice. The group most opposed weren't the high income earners, but those *just above* the current minimum wage level. They'd go from second-to-bottom to a last-placed-tie and they didn't want that.

Apart from last-place aversion, many others studies have shown that people can make seemingly illogical decisions based on relativity to other reference people or groups. Based on the table below, would you rather work for Company A or Company B?

A	B
You earn $60,000 and everyone else there earns $55,000	You earn $70,000 and everyone else there earns $75,000

Many studies have found that most people prefer to work for Company A despite earning less. Crazy yes? No, just human.

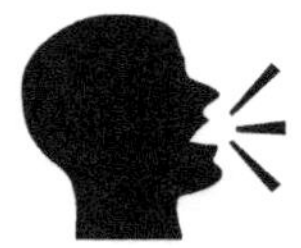

Loss Aversion

Daniel Kahneman and Amos Tversky's research found that people feel that the pain of a loss is twice that of the pleasure of a win. People have a negativity bias. It takes five good experiences to make up for a bad one. We place disproportionate weight on immediate gains and not enough on future costs. This greatly distorts our assessment of risk and therefore our behaviour. It limits us.

There's a tourist attraction in the Coromandel region of New Zealand called Waterworld. Part botanic gardens and part theme park, it features a large number of water-based installations that are fun, yet teach kids about water. Some generate power, some are used for playfights. While my kids were off swimming in the waterhole near the end of the park, I wandered off into a hedged-off area looking for somewhere flat and sunny to dry the towels. It was an oval garden area with a path around the perimeter. The gardens were nice but what was truly eye-catching was what was above it.

Dangling above the centre of the garden away from the path was a skeletal whale made out of pipes and hoses. It looked great – a robotic majesty. Where I stood on the path was this sign:

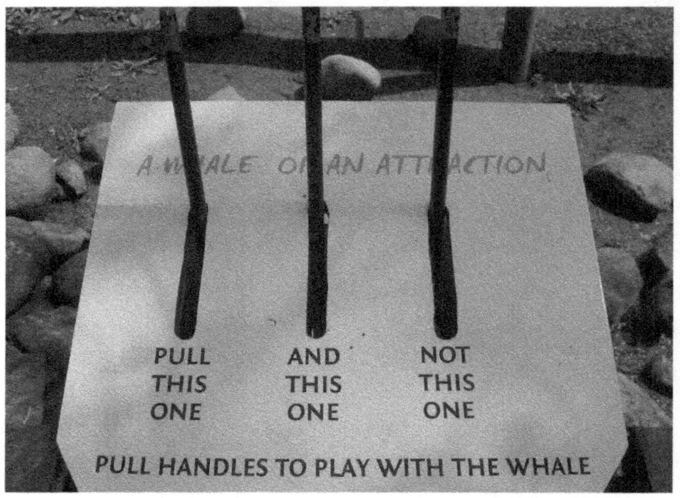

I pulled the first lever and the whale started moving in the air above me. I pulled the second lever and the whale started to spout a bit of water into the garden below. I pulled the third (and forbidden) lever and I was instantly drenched by the contents of a large tank hidden in the trees directly above me. I laughed til I cried, an uninhibited childlike giggling fit.

It was still quite early in the day and the whale area was empty so no one saw my dousing or giggling. I set up shop on a dry patch opposite and did a little survey. I counted the people who came in but who hadn't been witness to any third-lever drenching. How many of them would pull the third lever? How many do you think?

19%! This was a fun park not a steel mill. Has society become so risk averse that they won't take a tiny chance like that?

Stop →Think →Act

What does this idea mean for you personally?

What might this idea have to do with someone you lead?

Thinking about a particular person you lead, how might you encourage them towards more productive levels of risk taking?

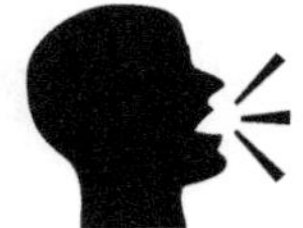

Choice

Psychologist Barry Schwartz did the groundwork on this topic. People value choice and try hard to get themselves into positions of choice but choices often undercut our happiness. Broadly, when it comes to choosers, people fall into one of two categories. Maximizers seek out the best possible choice. They make social comparisons, eventually make better choices on average but are less happy afterwards. Indeed, maximizers are more prone to depression generally. Satisficers are happy enough when good enough is good enough. They make less good choices but are happier afterwards.

Social psychologists Sheena Lyengar from Columbia University Business School and Mark Lepper from Stanford University conducted a famous study in 2000 that involved observing people at a jam stall offering samples and sales to passers-by. They showed that when shoppers are given the option of choosing among smaller and larger assortments of jam, they show more interest in the larger assortment. But when it comes time to pick just one, they're 10 times more likely to make a purchase if they choose among six rather than among 24 flavours of jam.

When faced with too large an array of choices, people are less likely to make any choice at all or, if they do, they feel less satisfied. After all, what are the odds, given the large numbers of choices, that you picked the best one? People are less confident, feel greater regret and bear a greater opportunity cost, particularly in lost time.

Yesterday I did my weekly grocery shopping. I counted the number of varieties of toothpaste available to me – 17. I keep getting the same variety, not because I think it's especially superior but because changing seems like awfully hard work. I'm prepared to work hard for a lot of reasons. That is not one of them. The research shows I'm not unusual. (I'm pretty sure I'm very unusual in lots of other ways but not in this regard.)

In case you're thinking jam buyers are simple folk who can't handle complexity, Lyengar did effectively the same study on investors. They looked at 800,000 employees from 647 companies investing their retirement savings, choosing between two and fifty-nine options. Referring to retirement plans in the U.S. (401Ks), Lyengar said, 'People are given enormous incentives to participate through tax shelters and employer matches. So, essentially, if you choose not to participate, you're throwing away free money'. Guess what many of the people with too many choices did? They threw away free money. With two choices, 75% took part, but when given 59 choices, only 60% did. The more options there were, the more cautious people were with their investment strategies.

What are we supposed to do about this? How are we supposed to guide those we lead to deal with choices? Social psychologist Alexander Chernev of Northwestern University's Kellogg School of Management's research suggests the best approach to avoid the problems that come with too many choices is to enter the decision-making process with an 'articulated preference'. You then accept the first choice that at least meets that preference. Yes there may be better options available but there is a cost attached to bothering to look.

I'm not suggesting that if your company is looking for many expensive new computers that you shouldn't test the market and receive and thoroughly assess a multitude of proposals. But when individuals are faced with choices, this is their human reaction. Schwartz says, 'You may do slightly less well objectively, but you'll feel better about the results'. And you spend your better feelings and all that time you save being more productive.

Baruch College researchers ran studies with fast food restaurants and vending machines. After adding healthier options to the choices available, sales of the *least healthy* options increased dramatically. It was as if the possibility that the diners could have chosen a healthy option gave them permission to celebrate with a fat and salt laden treat.

Stop →Think →Act

What does this idea mean for you personally?

What might this idea have to do with someone you lead?

Thinking about a particular person you lead, how might you tweak your style in dealing with them to be more effective?

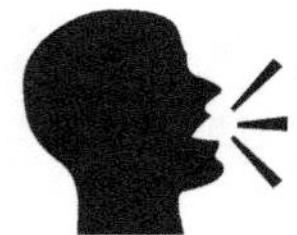

Relativity

Psychologist Dan Ariely in his book *Predictably Irrational* writes about an online advertisement for the British publication *The Economist*. It presented three subscription purchasing options:

Version	**Price**
Online Version	$US59
Print Version	$US125
Both Versions	$US125

If you were a fan of the magazine and were keen to buy, which option do you think you would prefer and why? You'd have to be crazy to buy just the 'Print' version when for zero dollars extra, you could get both the 'Print' AND 'Online' versions. Ariely did a study and here is what people chose:

Version	**Price**	**Chosen**
Online Version	$US59	16%
Print Version	$US125	0%
Both Versions	$US125	84%

Ariely did another study but *without* the relative option of the 'Print' version. Here's how those results compared to the results *with* the relative option of the 'Print' version:

Version	Price	Chosen
Online Version	$US59	68%
Print Version	$US125	Not available
Both Versions	$US125	32%

So, it seems the clever people at *The Economist* generate a great deal more revenue by the way they frame the relative information in their pricing structure. We like to think we're rational creatures making sound decisions based on the best information we have but reality suggests that we make an awful lot of decisions (or a lot of awful decisions) based on what we compare things to. And therefore an awful lot of influence can be generated by those who provide that information. In your workplace, that would be you.

Don't believe me? Run this fun little pop quiz with your friends or family based on studies done by Tversky & Kahneman. You're after a fancy pen. In the store you're in, it costs $25. Your smart phone tells you that five minutes away is a store that sells them for $18. Do you take that walk to save $7? Most people choose to take that walk. Now, you're after a suit. In the store you're in, it costs $500. Your smart phone tells you that five minutes away is a store that sells them for $493. Do you take that walk to save $7? Most people choose *not* to take that walk. Even after declaring that they would take the walk to save $7 earlier on the pen, most still say that they wouldn't to save the $7 on the suit.

Why not? $7 is $7 is $7, right? Nope! Once again, we make decisions based on relativity not rationality.

Which of the following situations do you think would make you happier?

Situation A	**Situation B**
Your Salary: $45000 Your Co-Worker's Salary: $35000	Your Salary: $50000 Your Co-worker's Salary: $60000

Most people opt for the Situation A. Despite being less, our happiness is boosted by our superior relativity to those around us.

Stop →Think →Act

What does this idea mean for you personally?

What might this idea have to do with someone you lead?

Thinking about a particular person you lead, how might you tweak your style in dealing with them to be more effective?

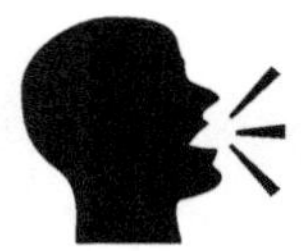

Making Requests

Psychologists Ellen Langer, Arthur Blank and Benzion Chanowitz ran a cute little study with a scenario that many of us will recognise at an emotional level – queue jumping. Using a queue for the photocopier at a library, they measured the relative influence of three requests to cut in front. They took two approaches, one with 5 copies (a small favour) and one with 20 copies (a large favour):

Request	
'Excuse me, I have 5/20 copies. May I use the copier?'	No reason
'Excuse me, I have 5/20 copies. May I use the copier because I have to make some copies?'	Placebo reason
'Excuse me, I have 5/20 copies. May I use the copier because I'm in a rush?'	Real reason

How many said, 'Yes'?

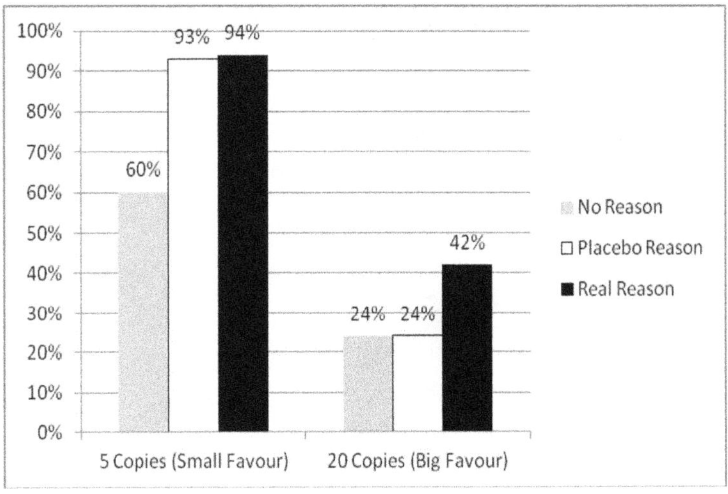

So, any reason has traction for a small favour but larger favours need a reason with some legitamcy. I was surprised as I think I would guard my place in the queue with ferocity or, at least, I think I would. That's not what the research says. A legit reason is no guarantee and doesn't even move half the population but it costs nothing and improves your odds. Bear that in mind when you think about telling someone to just bloody do something.

Stop →Think →Act

What does this idea mean for you personally?

What might this idea have to do with someone you lead?

Thinking about a particular person you lead, how might you tweak your style of giving directions and asking for things with them to be more effective?

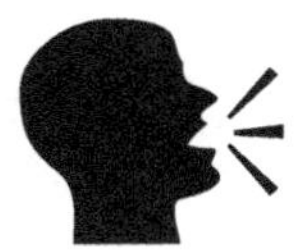

Setting Expectations

A simple example of framing in setting expectations is a study of doctors who routinely gave their patients a choice about optional surgery. Using one type of surgery as an example, some doctors told patients that this surgery had a 90% survival rate whereas some doctors said it had a 10% mortality rate. (The logical risk is identical in both phrasings.) Acceptance of the offers framed as 90% survival was 84%. Acceptance of the offers framed as 10% mortality was 50%.

If you're running a power company, should you penalise customers who pay late or reward those who pay early? If you're an environmentalist trying to promote the use of energy-efficient light bulbs, should you say that using them could save you $200 a year or that not using them could lose you $200 a year? Each choice makes no difference to the power company or the environmentalist, yet people perceive the offers quite differently. Remember loss aversion? It's even more influential when combined with framing.

Reframing is effortful and our brain is lazy. Control the frame and you greatly influence people's understanding and expectations of upcoming situations.

Have you been to the supermarket recently and seen any offers akin to 5-for-$5? Even if situations where they've trialled offers like this with the individual unit price at 1-for-$1, the 5-for-$5 offer results in average sales increases of 32%. Bear in mind this is for situations where there is no actual true saving to be made by bulk-buying. That's framing at work again.

A study done in an Edinburgh supermarket by Adrian North of Heriot Watt University looked at, or rather listened to, music played in their wine department. Playing French music increased sales of French wines and playing German music increased sales of German wine. Another study showed classical music improved wine sales but Top 40 music hurt them. There was even some evidence that music primed wine drinkers' perception of taste. I can think of heavy music and mellow music but I'd have to check out my iTunes to see if I have any music with earthy tones or hints of citrus. Maybe *ColdPlay*?

Be very aware of the words you use, your reasons for using them and the impact they may have. Don't be a victim to your vocabulary's accidental evolution over time. Take deliberate control over it. Elizabeth Loftus of the University of Washington ran some studies that showed participants videos of car accidents. Afterwards, they were split into groups and each group was asked pretty much the same question. The only difference was that the researcher would use a different word to describe how the cars crashed into each other. This is the question below, with the variable word left blank:

> 'About how fast were the cars going when
> they _______ into each other?'

The table below shows the variable words used and the effect on the estimates of the participants:

Word	**Average Speed Estimate**
'smashed'	40.8mph
'collided'	39.3mph
'bumped'	38.1mph
'hit'	34.0mph
'contacted'	31.8mph

Stop →Think →Act

What does this idea mean for you personally?

What might this idea have to do with someone you lead?

Thinking about a particular person you lead, how might you tweak your style in dealing with them to be more effective?

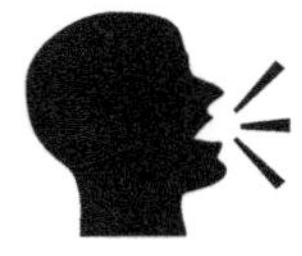

One Reason People See Things Differently

Get three buckets. Fill one with water at room temperature. Fill one with icy cold water. Fill the third with water hot enough for a bath. Pop one of your bare feet into the cold bucket and the other into the hot bucket. Wait a minute then put both feet into the room temperature bucket. Your cold bucket foot perceives the new bucket as warm whereas your hot bucket foot perceives the new bucket as cool. It's the same bucket! Try it with the kids. It blows their minds.

It's also a nice little metaphor for how people perceive things after being strongly influenced by what's just happened.

If you're going to call one of your team into your office for a chat, their reaction to that invitation and the subsequent chat will be influenced by what happened immediately beforehand. To what extent can you influence that to everyone's advantage?

Stop →Think →Act

What does this idea mean for you personally?

What might this idea have to do with someone you lead?

Thinking about a particular person you lead, how might you tweak your style in dealing with them to be more effective?

Keeping Motivation Going

How many coffee shop loyalty cards do you have? (If you have more than one, you may wish to consult a dictionary for the meaning of the word '*loyalty*'.) Do they all operate in the same way? Think about all the old-fashioned loyalty cards you've seen. Not the new electronic point-collecting plastic cards with magnetic strips or microchips. Think of the timeless dog-earred cardboard ones with ten squares or cups or whatever and purchases that earned a stamp or a hole punch. At some delicious and delirious future time, you get that tenth stamp and the next cup is FREE!!! It's like Christmas but without the immense tension, family drama and homicidal/suicidal thoughts.

Did those cards affect your behaviour? Did they drive your decision-making? In what ways? Which type of cards were most successful – *for the cafe*? The whole point of those things, one would presume, was to increase profit in the long run for the cafe. They're not giving you free coffee because you're awesome. (This in no way belittles your actual level of awesomeness.)

In 2006, a study was done at a car wash contrasting two different approaches to loyalty cards. Half the cards were normal 'get eight stamps, get one free' cards. The other half were the same except that the card needed TEN stamps but the first two stamps had already been given. For that second group of cards, the first purchase was, in effect, the **THIRD** stamp. For the business, the cost was the same for both types of card – the customer still needed to buy eight car washes.

And this had what impact?

19% of the first group of cards got redeemed up to the tenth and final stamp thus rewarding the customer their freebie. And how did the second group of cards go? 34%! Almost double. AND they filled their cards quicker AND as they got closer to completing their card, the gaps between car washes diminished. The closer they got to their 'goal', the more active they appeared to be pursuing it.

That's interesting in and of itself if you're running a business and considering implementing a loyalty card. That's not what I'm writing about though. This is just a demonstration of a good old predictable human trait called 'Endowed Progress'. People are more likely to progress towards a goal if they perceive they have already made progress towards it.

How can we help others move towards their work and life goals leveraging the endowed progress effect? Weight loss or a promotion are common goals, although both would be better expressed using something like the SMART model. (Specific, measurable, attainable, relevant and time-bound. 'Lose 10kg in 3 months etc'.) Somehow they need to give themselves credit for the progress they've already made before they officially start. The weight-loss equivalent of two free stamps.

Conversely, people can experience negative effects with endowed progress. Ever waited for a bus? The bus is late. The bus is later still. Maybe the bus isn't coming at all? Again, research indicates that the more time we invest in waiting for something, the more irrationally attached we become to continue waiting. (That said, *you just know* that the moment you walk *just far enough* away, the bus will come around the corner… psych!!)

Stop →Think →Act

What does this idea mean for you personally?

What might this idea have to do with someone you lead?

Thinking about a particular person you lead, how might you guide them into giving themselves credit for any endowed progress they've made towards their goals?

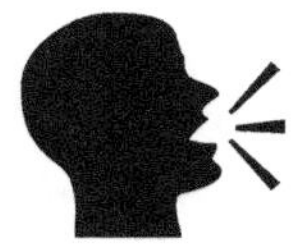

Conformity

Doctor Nicholas Christaki of the Harvard Medical School concluded that we are 171% more likely to gain weight if our closest friends do. We don't even have to be geographically close, just emotionally close. He describes this as 'an emotional contagion'.

Sunstein and Thaler write about a study conducted in restaurants measuring how much individuals eat when in groups of different sizes:

Group Size	Impact On Average Individual Consumption
1	--
2	+35%
4	+75%
7+	+96%

Slow down people; it is not a contest.

Solomon Asch back in the 1950s conducted some classic trials on conformity. It was a series where everyone was in on it except the actual participant. People were put into groups of five to seven people. All but one of the group were confederates of the researcher. The group was shown a card with a line on it, then another card with three lines on it of differing lengths. Everyone was then asked which line matched the length of the line on the first card. They had three rounds of this activity. In the first two rounds, all the confederates gave the correct (and quite obvious) answer, as did the subject. In the third round, the confederates, as scripted, gave an obviously incorrect answer. 37% of the subjects gave the wrong answer, agreeing with the blatantly wrong confederates of the researcher. This compared to a control group of people where the wrong answer was given 1% of the time.

Online retailers will tell you that other people who bought what you just bought, also bought these other three items. *People just like you.* The movie website IMDB and others will let you rate movies and based on your assessments, recommend other movies to you based on the ratings of *people just like you.*

The flipside of social proof is social projection, where what's going on in your world distorts your view of the world outside. People who are having relationship problems notice evidence (or think they do) of discord in everyone else's relationships.

As long as I'm talking flipsides, let look at a downside – social loafing. Have you ever been peer pressured into a tug-of-war contest at a company picnic or school fair? You must have helped someone shift house at some point. Maybe it took two or three people to carry the big fridge or couch? Did you get the feeling that maybe not everyone was giving it their maximum effort? That's social loafing in action. (Um, inaction.)

Max Ringelmann's research has shown that this may be caused by a diffusion of responsibility. If there's any blame, it gets divided up. At work, the age-old practice of group brainstorming is actually less effective as most members coast. Other methods can allow for and lessen that effect.

Stop →Think →Act

What does this idea mean for you personally?

What might this idea have to do with someone you lead?

Thinking about a particular person you lead, how might you tweak your style in dealing with them to be more effective?

Section Three

Becoming A Brain-Based Boss

What Can Volunteers Teach Us About Creating A Motivated Workplace?

'When you cease to make a contribution, you begin to die.'
– Eleanor Roosevelt

In his book *The Blue Zone: Lessons for living longer from the people who've lived the longest*, Dan Buettner reveals his studies of four pockets of population around the world where people routinely live beyond one hundred years of age with a decent quality of life. He distils down to nine ingredients what's so special about these people and these places. It's not the air or the water or the radiation from a crash-landed alien spacecraft. It's a set of specific lifestyle habits – choices the people there make, or had imposed on them by chance but choose to continue.

1. Just move. They don't pump iron or run marathons but they move constantly.
2. Purpose now. A reason to get up in the morning.
3. Down shift. Routines to help relieve stress.
4. 80%. Eat til you're not hungry rather than full.
5. Plant slant. Make meat the side dish.

6. Wine at 5.00 pm with friends, that's the trick.
7. Belong. Some kind of faith.
8. Loved ones first. Focus on family and relationships.
9. Right tribe. Supportive social circles.

The Blue Zone is about living a longer, active and more meaningful life. What has this got to do with leading workplaces and the people in them to becoming more successful? Point number two of Buettner's list is *having a purpose*, a reason to get up in the morning. That certainly came through strongly within my own research into volunteers.

I started talking to people who led formal groups of volunteers because they struck me as a proving ground for many of the principles I discovered in researching this book. It's all very well for me to suggest that a workforce abundant with self awareness, mastery, autonomy, purpose and influencing others will lead to greater success. Money isn't on that list but, try as I and others might to downplay the cash, it is still a significant component of why people seek and stay in employment. Not necessarily employment with you but employment generally. But money doesn't mean they'll be especially productive when they arrive at their job. What if we removed the money from the equation and looked at situations where people sought, showed up for and strived at an activity that, for all intents and purposes, was a job, except for *a complete lack of pay*?

Volunteers. I'm not talking about spending a few hours collecting for charity or running a barbeque outside a shopping centre for the swim club. I'm not talking about volunteers who coach kids' sports or do the club paperwork. I'm talking about people who show up on a regular, formally scheduled basis to perform specified tasks with other people with defined outcomes, standards and so forth. You know, like a job. But for free.

I spoke with people who lead lifeguards, corporate hospitality, tourism information centres and fundraising for children with life threatening illnesses. Because of the nature of their work and their ongoing relationships with their current and future volunteers, they have asked, and I have agreed, not to name them or their organisations.

Before beginning my observations of their operations with their people and my discussions with them, I first gave them an overview of the angle I was taking. What do employers who actually pay their employees have to learn from organisations who do not pay their workers? How do you attract, retain, motivate and develop people and collectively succeed when volunteers can leave at any time for any reason with zero consequences for themselves? These organisations had the same organisational needs as a profit-making company or government department, yet few, if any, had the traditional carrots and sticks that a paying employer would have.

The provider of corporate hospitality was a profit-making company that sponsored a motor racing team. Their volunteers were drawn from their own paid staff, often quite senior, who went unpaid for their efforts providing frontline service at motor racing events like bartending and rubbish collection – quite 'non-senior' activities. I worked alongside them for three seasons and some of the work was very hard. Packing in and packing out a bus full of large awnings, flooring and equipment into tricky and uneven terrain beside race tracks was hard work, physically and mentally, with most tasks needing close teamwork and a focus on the health and safety of ourselves and clients.

The company was owned overseas and had a very flat organisational structure. There were no political or 'brownie' points to be scored by volunteering. Not all of them were even that enthralled by motor racing itself. Why then did they do it and how did it work?

Before I answer that, let me outline the other volunteer-based operations I looked at because the answers to the 'why' and the 'how' were remarkably similar in all of them. If you've read this far into this book, you'll also find that the answers to the 'why' and the 'how' of formally managing volunteers align consistently with the five principles of self awareness, mastery, autonomy, purpose and influencing others. The four operations were quite different, yet their approaches to formally managing volunteers were almost identical.

One was a profit-making company using volunteers as hospitality providers on the weekends to effectively enhance the company's relationship with their profit-providing client base who enjoyed motor racing. One was a very professional international fundraising not-for-profit delivering 'magic' to children with life threatening illnesses. One was a Governmental agency providing tourist information staffed predominantly by older citizens. One was mostly crewed by young people training other young people to save lives and maintain safety within a competitive sporting environment. What could these groups possibly have in common?

One commonality and evidence of the success of all four groups was that their volunteer force was over-subscribed. For unpaid hard work, there was more demand to do the work than there was supply of volunteer vacancies. It wasn't always the case, it did fluctuate and the price of that success was constant vigilance. The first thing that struck me about all of the organisations was how formal and organised they all were. My uninformed impression going in was that they would be informal and ad hoc but the complete opposite was true. Indeed, their success relied heavily upon detailed and deep organisation. Having people choosing to work for you for free doesn't happen by accident.

Be they paid or unpaid, organisations need to attract workers. The volunteer groups almost solely sourced their people via pre-existing networks or social connections, usually the volunteers themselves. Who better knows if someone is going to be a good fit, willing and able to do a volunteer role, than someone who is already doing it? A phrase I heard often was 'in the loop,' although one I preferred was 'plugging them into our matrix'. Think back to our chapter on employee engagement, one of the dead giveaways of active engagement was a lack of hesitation in recommending this place to your friends as a great place to work. The volunteer organisations didn't just consider this as one of a number of options – it was the main and almost sole option because it was their most successful and effective method. They didn't have to run ads in the classifieds to attract volunteers. This method didn't just attract applicants to make up numbers, it attracted applicants with 'Functional Fit'(defined later in this section) who stayed for productive lengths of time. How true is that for you with job adverts and other mainstream traditional methods of attracting paid employees?

This 'matrix' that volunteers were being plugged into provided them potentially with a sense of purpose, a structure and sense of belonging that they weren't getting currently elsewhere in their lives. The lifeguards were young. The tourist information people were largely retired from 'real' jobs. Three of the four managers described their operation as 'like family,' which, again, is something many people lack a true sense of in their lives. This sense of 'familyness' doesn't happen by accident. (This technique is also used by organised crime gangs.)

They all deliberately cultivated an environment of reciprocated commitment which, if you leave bloodlines out of it, is probably a large part of defining what a family is. Lots of bosses send a card around and collect a bit of petty cash for a birthday in paid workplaces but it needs to be a lot more than that in a volunteer environment and it needs to be formally organised. I was astonished at the depth and detail they went into.

All organisations kept files on individual volunteers noting their birthdays, anniversaries and other details of special and *personal* significance. Diary systems operated to ensure these were appropriately recognised on time, regardless of who was on duty at the time. Laminated job aids were displayed on the walls of their tea rooms so that everyone's individual tea and coffee preferences were tracked and supplied. When you ain't getting paid, tea and coffee take on a disproportionate importance. It's easy, cheap and returns the effort many times over.

Lots of managers of paid employees say they try and get to know their people. In all honesty, really getting to know someone involves writing down details and implementing systems. Otherwise it relies on managers' memories and spare time, neither of which is reliable at all.

Reciprocated commitment is more than birthdays and cookies. It's when tough times hit that the commitment test gets tested. The volunteer managers made a point of hospital visits, attending funerals and staying in touch even with volunteers who had left the loop.

The point of this, at a superficial level, was the message of support it sent to the recipient of the birthday wish or the hospital visit. There were other benefits in maintaining contact with past volunteers. They proved to be a hot source of funds, information, connections and more volunteers down the track. Of greatest value to the organisation was the message it sent to everyone else still in the volunteer force – you are *like family*...

All managers of the volunteers had started out themselves as volunteers, so they were always able to see things from the volunteers' point of view. As we'll see shortly in the chapter about being 'autonomy supportive', one of the signs of being an autonomy supportive manager is instinctively answering questions about your employees from their point of view.

Volunteers tended to be one of two types. Either they, or someone in their inner circle of friends and family, were really passionate about the subject, or they were in the market to volunteer for 'something' but they weren't sure what. There was real talent in this second group so the managers of volunteers were deliberate in differentiating themselves from other volunteering options and doing so consistently. They didn't just say what they thought potential volunteers wanted to hear. They were willing to have vacant roles rather than simply populating them because they could. Of critical importance to all the managers was a concept they called 'Functional Fit'.

Functional fit described a greater focus on fitting in with the current volunteer personnel and the values of the organisation than on any technical skills or experience the volunteer applicants might have. All the organisations were detailed and open with applicants about what they stood for, how they differed from other volunteer organisations and what their processes and expectations were. 'No surprises,' was a common catch-cry and yet another definitive lesson from volunteers for paid employers. If you want people who will engage, add value and stick around, they need to be functionally fit above all else.

Given the volunteers were unpaid, I asked if they ever received gifts or similar tangible forms of rewards. Those organisations that had tried it no longer chose to use it. Remember back to our Swedish blood donors who stopped donating once they started getting paid? Cash and tangible gifts turn volunteerism into a transaction and kills much of the drive behind their engagement. Saving lives for free is a noble calling; patrolling a cold, windswept beach for a personalised coffee mug and a token gift of petrol vouchers makes you a schmuck.

Managers had mixed views when it came to intangible forms of reward and recognition. Apart from a sense of belonging, purpose and structure, of feeling like part of something 'like family' within an environment of reciprocated commitment, some people were after other returns from their volunteering. Some of these seemed, on the surface, to be positive but the grizzled voices of experience of the managers told me otherwise.

Going in, I thought that many volunteers would do so for the feeling of helping out others and that this was a good thing. The experienced managers told me of how there is a big difference between *feeling* like you're helping others and actually doing so.

Some volunteers, though seemingly altruistic, were strongly driven by 'bragging rights' and ego association ('Look at me helping the sick kids everyone'). All but one of the groups had formal written agreements with their volunteers which were very similar to what an employee might think of as a 'contract.' Health and safety, pre-existing health conditions, privacy, and so forth need to be worried about by volunteer managers as if they were paid employees. On top of those were some volunteer-specific issues obviously born out of the pain of past experience. One agreement limited what people could say in their CVs about their work with the group. Another prevented signees from uploading or tagging images on social networking sites of them during their volunteer activities. (So, no, you can't look at me with the sick kid and rightly so, when you think about it.)

Visual evidence of inclusion and structure were effective tools. The one thing volunteers in all four groups pointed me at were photos of teams past and present. Even in the hustle and bustle of the day's motor racing, time was always religiously allocated so everyone could get into the team photo. The drivers themselves identified the value volunteers felt in the photos and made considerable efforts to be there to take part.

Nevertheless, recognition was often required and fair enough too. All stressed the importance of reinforcing the right things. The number one aspect managers sought more of and therefore praised and recognised was *effort,* rather than numbers or results. Remember Carol Dweck's experiments with fixed versus growth mindsets?

The volunteer group that was least like the others was the motor racing hospitality providers. They had paid day jobs and had precious little discretionary time, yet volunteered anyway. Some were 'petrol heads' into motor racing for its own sake, but most weren't. Most were in quite senior roles yet volunteered for very junior-type tasks. These events required travel not to tropical vacation destinations but small towns' dusty racetracks and basic motels, yet they volunteered anyway. No one interviewed really thought they were enhancing their career prospects by volunteering. What was in it for these people?

They got the same things that the non-corporate volunteers got:

- A feeling of functional fitness which most jobs rarely give you all the time if any of the time.
- Invitation/inclusion and differentiation.
- A sense of purpose, structure and belonging.
- 'Familyness' – reciprocated commitment.
- Not just part of something but part of something that is obviously well organised with a clear goal.
- Receiving timely and customised feedback with recognition of effort.
- Leadership sharing their point of view and generally sharing an experience with a proven track record of positive outcomes.

One difference between this group and the others was that their volunteers were given much more autonomy than just being in an 'autonomy supportive' environment. In fact, often and deliberately, more junior team members were given leadership roles over people technically higher up the food chain back at the office. I'm not pretending for a moment this always worked out first time. Often it didn't. But it always worked out. This new dynamic to their professional relationship added value to the individuals concerned and to the company as whole too. Better to work out how to deal with friction with an executive over who was supposed to refill the ice bucket than over the loss of a major client at work.

Year after year, the good news stories and gossip over the frictions all did the rounds of the grapevine and the watercoolers. Despite this, or perhaps because of this, not once in ten years has the corporate's operational manager ever had to ask for volunteers. They all self submit or get volunteered by others. However, there's something too in being offered up by someone else for a select role, even as a volunteer, that makes people commit more firmly.

The manager commented, 'One trading bank in this country makes a big deal in its advertising that 'we donate one day per year for each of our staff to plant trees.' I doubt many of their staff would plant trees if that day was deducted from their annual leave.' I suspect he's right.

Here are some broad guidelines for dealing with volunteers. As you read them, consider how many are equally applicable to a paid workforce situation:

- Set ambitious goals.
- Be organised (Don't waste their time).
- Enable them to fulfil their needs (unless they have some that aren't compatible with yours).
- Ensure paid staff actively show that they appreciate the volunteers.
- Provide regular customised feedback.
- Proximity equals likeability.
- Provide customised recognition.
- Inclusion (Invite them in).

I need to make one final mention of volunteers filling a gap they had in their working or personal lives – quality feedback. Providing this in a regular and meaningful way was far more important, effective and less costly than throwaway gifts. On the subject of feedback, one manager used the term 'Hunger.' Another said, 'Addiction.'

Feedback enhances *self awareness*. Volunteering enables people to learn new skills or keep their hand in at existing ones supporting people moving towards *mastery*. Having leaders with a shared point of view stimulates an *autonomy* supportive environment. The 'no surprises' policy and differentiation strategy makes volunteer organisations sense of *purpose* obvious. Ultimately that purpose when volunteering is about positively and effectively influencing others.

Leaders of paid employees can learn a lot from those leading volunteer workforces. I know I did.

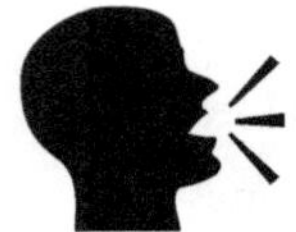

Recruiting

A phrase I've heard a lot of managers utter but not necessarily follow is, 'Recruit for attitude, Train for skill'. I get what they mean. You can cause a lot of costs, delays and heartache for a lot of people by employing the wrong person in the wrong job in the wrong team at the wrong time. If you've got a choice of similarly qualified people as far as technical skills go, but someone's got a better attitude then it's wiser to trade off and hire the person with the better attitude. You can always up their skills but it's hard or impossible to change anyone's attitude. This is what these people say.

I understand all that but the problem I have is with this 'attitude' thing of which they speak. What's that? What does it look and sound like? Apparently there are good ones and bad ones. You can't see an attitude. You can only see evidence of it – behaviour. And it's evidence of behaviour you should be looking for during your recruitment processes. A structured interview technique will help you identify, challenge and validate behaviours that demonstrate your applicant might have their brain in the right place.

The questions below aren't questions you'd ask applicants directly, but they are questions you need answered in order to find out whether these people would help you as a brain-based boss. You need to phrase the questions yourself in order to suit the particular workplace situations. For example, you cannot ask a question like, 'Are you self disciplined?' No one is ever going to answer, 'No'. A better question for an applicant might be, 'Tell me about a time you took over a call that required some self discipline on your part? What happened and how did it turn out?' Keep them on track so they answer about specific things they themselves did (behaviours).

- Do they run their own minds?
- Are they self disciplined?
- Are they creative?
- Can they organise?
- How do they solve problems?
- To what extent do they think about their own performance?
- Evidence of self motivation/perseverance.
- Evidence of wanting to achieve.
- Evidence of good relationships.
- Evidence of overcoming resistance.

Basketball geeks who follow the NBA love a statistic called the 'Plus/Minus'. Broadly speaking, this summarises the overall impact each player has on the team while they are on the court. A player who scores a lot might be deficient in other areas of performance, much as a sales rep for a company might be great at making sales but causes costs and problems in other aspects of their work. Maybe the star scorer makes others around them worse and maybe that's true of the star sales rep too? The Plus/Minus rates and weights all the information available and gives you a snapshot at a certain point in time of whether the performer is either worth it or not. You're probably not looking to hire a point guard. You might be looking to hire an engineer. They may have splendid technical engineering skills and experience but what is the most objective evidence of their overall 'Plus/Minus'?

Brain-Based Boss Seed Of An Idea

Update your questions you use in your structured employment interviews. Ask, 'Tell me about a time when you had to defer something to put yourself in a position for a better result later on.' Let's see what evidence they can provide of self discipline characteristics and marshmallow delaying...

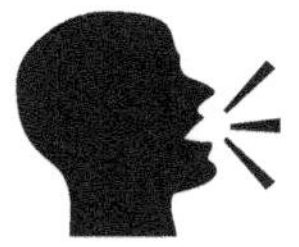

Orientation/Induction

Invest time wisely with new employees. This is where their engagement is often lost. Few people start a job pre-disengaged. If they do, you might want to re-read the section on recruitment.

Spend time with them on the job. You'll get to understand them better as individuals. You'll see how they handle the job. This helps you deal with problems before they become PROBLEMS. In these situations, and if conflict arises, deal with the feelings first then the problem. (Remember the anablep.) They'll get to know you. There are opportunities, both ways, for feedback. With feedback, focus on one thing at a time. It encourages the flow of ideas and opinions. It's a chance to explain and encourage the alignment of their individual goals with your wider workplace or organisational goals. Look like you're actively listening. Write stuff down. This time upfront sets the stage for your relationship as the employees develop. Remember, 70% of the times people leave their job, it is not the job they choose to get away from, it is their boss. The best predictor of an employee's satisfaction with their boss is *frequency of interaction.*

One thing that'll differentiate you from the bulk of workaday non-brain-based bosses is a greater synching of expectations and perceptions with your people. In most workplaces, there are huge gaps. Alan Fairweather, in his book *How To Be A Motivational Manager*, cites the oft-quoted study showing how differently managers and employees value different employee satisfaction influencers:

Influencer	**Managers' Ranking**	**Employees' Ranking**
Job security	2	4
Sympathetic understanding	9	9
Company loyalty to employees	7	8
Interesting work	5	1
Good working conditions	4	7
Tactful discipline	6	10
Fair salary	1	5
Growth & promotion opportunities	3	6
A feeling of contributing	10	3
Appreciation for work done	8	2

Be 'Autonomy Supportive'

I don't agree with leaders who think that people should just do their bloody jobs that they're paid to do and stop whinging, but I don't want you to think for a moment that I'm suggesting leaders should step back from being firm and decisive and let anyone do anything anytime they feel like it. 'Autonomy supportive' is not a euphemism for gutless permissiveness. Everyone still needs to achieve results, do their job and work together. Leaders need to be there removing obstacles and providing resources, direction and feedback. But how can you best do that and still provide people as much as practicable with their natural need for autonomy? And, again, is it worth it?

Yes it is worth it. Deci's study of Xerox employees showed that employees with an 'autonomy supportive' manager were more trusting of the company, less concerned about pay and had higher job satisfaction and morale.

Workers who are anxious, for whatever reason, are more focused and on-task but are highly risk-averse. That might be a good thing depending on their role. However, they rely more on habit and routine and are less creative. That might be a bad thing depending on their role. Non-anxious workers are more explorative, see the bigger picture not just the narrow focus on the particular task at the time, take acceptable risks and are more creative.

You may not use the term autonomy supportive to describe yourself but maybe you are already. How can you tell? One clue that a manager may be autonomy supportive is when you ask them about an employee and they reply from *the employee's point of view*. How do you answer when asked about your people?

What do autonomy supportive leaders do? They avoid controlling language. They align themselves with the point of view of the person being limited, not necessarily aligning themselves with that person but understanding their perspective. They recognise any proactivity coming from the other person and encourage more of it. Instead of instantly criticising or critiquing poor performance, they ask what the performer's thoughts are about the incident.

How To Effectively Provide Support – 'Scaffolding'

Psychologist Lev Semyonovich Vygotsky compared a supportive workplace environment to the scaffolding he would see used on building sites. It gets put up to provide access and support as building occurs. Only what is needed gets provided and when it is no longer needed, it is removed.

Leigh Branham's antidote for employers to his seven hidden reasons employees leave revolves around meeting the expectations of applicants, communicating differently to different people, taking better care of new hires, giving supervisors the freedom and training to manage people their own way and embracing the belief that good employees can leave for the right reasons with new skills and good will and that's a good thing.

Branham promotes an 'Employer of choice scorecard' measuring and publicising:

- Voluntary staff turnover.
- Referral rates.
- Ratio of internal hires.
- New hire retention.
- Engagement.
- Absenteeism.

It's a fine line between allowing the privilege of autonomy and abdicating responsibility. Thirty years ago, I worked my way through university at a building supply warehouse. This was in the mid 1980s and workplace safety hadn't been invented yet as far as I could tell. Starting out sweeping up, I ended up doing all the selling and delivering that the permanent guys did. Apart from my lack of body fat and cigarettes, I blended right in. For the most part, I thought I had the skills sorted too. What I didn't have, technically, was the paperwork such as a legal driving licence for some of the equipment used around the store like overhead cranes, heavy trucks and forklifts. As I said, it was the mid 1980s so society had to put up with *Wham*, *Miami Vice* and me driving trucks without a licence.

One day in my third year I must have earned quite a few trust points with the managers as an important training session was being run for the fulltime staff and I was left in sole charge of the store during a slow part of the day. This was a multi-laned drive-through hardware warehouse with wallboards and all the big stuff, not just a shop with the bits and pieces. Out the back all the lanes ended up in the yard where we kept the steel and so forth. Deliveries would arrive in the yard and we'd unload the trucks then double-handle the goods into the store. Inefficient I know but that's the way things were done around there.

It was quiet during the training session until a truck arrived with a delivery of particle board flooring. These were big packs. Each sheet was 3.6 metres by 1.8 metres and weighed 100 kilograms by itself. There were 10 sheets in a pack. I had unloaded these before using our in-house forklift. The drivers are always in a hurry and time is money so we'd take them off two packs at a time. Once you lifted them up fractionally off the truck, you needed to tilt the forks back just a bit so you could reverse away from the truck and lower them from the two to three metres they were off the ground. I'd done it before and while there was little margin for error, I didn't hesitate in expressing my autonomy and deciding to unload the truck.

Unbeknownst to me, with Christmas approaching, the factory had embarked on a Christmas sales promotion, adding two extra bonus sheets to each pack at no extra cost. That's a real bargain – a *400 kilogram bargain.* I went through my tested procedure for unloading and it went fine. The forklift was quite powerful, albeit a little short in the fork department. Things went fine with the lifting. It was the little tilt back that sent things awry.

The extra 400 kilograms made a difference. Instead of remaining on the forks as it had always done before, the tilt back caused a wobble and the laws of physics being what they were in the mid 1980s, the 2.4 tonne, 1.8 metre wide load of flooring tilted *the other way* – over the *front* end of my 1.2 metre forks!

The entire load kept on in that direction, disappearing over the far edge of the truck I was unloading. It fell edge down onto the ashphalt on the other side of the truck. There was another truck parked on the other side and, miraculously, because it was falling edge-ways it missed both trucks almost entirely. It barely clipped a wing mirror on the way down. (I noticed this because time had slowed down for me.) Particle board is good for cheap flooring for cheap houses. It ain't pretty to look at but it's solid enough. It's called particle board because it's basically just saw-dust and chips of leftover wood super-glued together. Laid flat it can take a lot of weight and force. It has to; it's a floor. What it's *not* designed to do is drop sideways from three metres above the ground with twenty three other sheets onto solid ground. The moment it struck, it disintegrated. Those scenes in movies where the building collapses and the hero crawls out covered in debris with that wide-eyed panda look – that was me. I had been wearing safety goggles because, you know, I cared about safety.

In my untrustworthy memory I am sure the dust erupted into a spectacular mushroom cloud and the whole thing was surprisingly quiet. The training course inside proceeded uninterrupted. At this point, I exercised my autonomy to make sure the driver was still alive and suggested to him that I wouldn't be signing the delivery receipt anytime soon. He laughed and I'm pretty sure he put in a good word for me with the bosses. I kept my job which funded my first degree, and that ultimately led to me being qualified and experienced enough to write this book.

And I learned a very valuable lesson about the power and limits of worker autonomy.

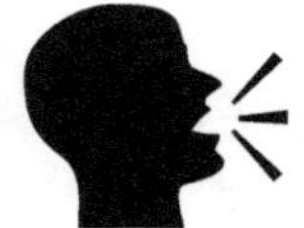

Conflict

For about five seconds I thought I'd invented the phrase 'Go ugly early'. Nope. There have been three previous popular uses for the term. It was code during prohibition at secret speakeasies when asked what time the booze would be around. 'Come pretty late' was translated to its opposite, 'Go ugly early.' (This is just one of many things I learned while watching *Boardwalk Empire*.) Secondly, sleazy guys trying to pick up women did some maths and worked out that the later the night went, the lower the chances of scoring the supposedly hotter women. (There are graphs, seriously. I guess they had plenty of time on their hands.) The more realistic sleazoids decide to 'go ugly early'. (I'm not approving, just noting the language.) I've even heard it used when a politician or celebrity has done something naughty and it's about to hit the headlines. Rather than wait for the news to be drip-fed over days, prolonging the damage and embarrassment, wise PR folk advise them to 'go ugly early' and get it all out at once. Damage is time multiplied by embarrassment. Minimise the time and lessen the damage.

So what?

Do you rip or peel off the bandaid? I deliver a lot of training to frontline supervisors. A common hesitation amongst them when starting out is to deal with conflict. My advice always is to go ugly early. Better to deal with conflict pimples than conflict volcanoes.

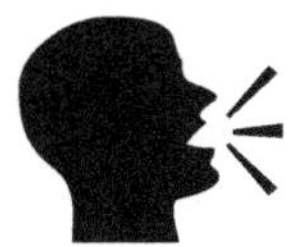

Work Stories

We've already learned that verbal persuasion and logical argument aren't particularly effective in the long run when it comes to modifying the behaviour of others. One technique to increase your chances of success with your talking is to use structured stories. Storytelling without the structure might make you some friends but there's no evidence it changes behaviour.

A structured workplace story needs these elements:

- Make them identify with the central character of the story as someone they know or someone *just like them*.
- Whatever happens to the central character could happen, or has happened, to them.
- Stimulate empathy.
- Include a solution (to fire up those mirror neurons).
- Answer the two critical questions:
    a. Is it worth it?
    b. Can I do it?

As a leader, you're trying to create modifications in behaviour by helping others change their mental maps of cause and effect. The story provides evidence that the solved problem is possible and desirable.

Chip and Dan Heath provide a timeless approach to communicating ideas in their book *Made To Stick* that's equally applicable to leadership stories as it is to marketing or urban legends.

They open with one such legend, that of a friend of a friend waking up in an Asian hotel room in a bath of ice with a cellphone, a note and one less kidney. That's never happened but, man oh man, does that story stick. Why? They've analysed many such success examples of stickiness and the common factors are:

- Simplicity.
- Unexpectedness.
- Concreteness.
- Credibility.
- Emotional content.
- Story.

It doesn't matter if it's a child's fairy tale or a real-life example of why workplace safety is critical, we need to communicate it in a way that makes it as effective as possible.

Tell the story from the point of view of the character with whom they'd identify. Break patterns to grab attention. People have a need for closure. (Remember the Zeigarnik Efect?) Open then close loops. Leave threads hanging until the end. Maybe get them to commit to a prediction as this drives engagement. Invoke self interest with phrases like, 'Imagine yourself...'. Avoid the trap of abstraction by using specific objects with which they're familiar. Don't talk about masses, talk about individuals like them. (Remember the power of one.)

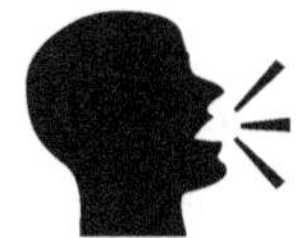

Turning Attention Into Action

The basic building block of comedy is the 'gag'. And the most common traditional gag is the one-liner which counter-intuitively is almost always made up of at least three lines: the premise, the setup and the punch. (This does have tangible business benefits I promise you.) Example: I live in a supermarket. The showers are great. Although, you do have to move the lettuces.

It's not the greatest gag in the world but it clearly is comprised of premise, setup and punch. Many of you will have heard the term punchline – the last line of a gag which makes it funny. Pro comedians take it further with the punch*word.* The later you can leave your reveal, the more dramatic and effective it is. In the case of a gag, misdirection plus a late reveal equals funny. The same principle can apply to business communication. In sales, if you've got a killer bit of compelling info, save it up for a reveal and create a context that makes your reveal even more dramatic.

Here's a real life example. I was MCing an HR conference. The room was full of decision makers – CEOs and HR Managers. The speaker was a forensic pathologist. Personally, I found her backstory incredibly interesting but then she wasn't trying to sell to me. After some CSI-like stories from the 1970s, she spoke of working her way up from scientist to manager and was pitching to this audience the value of workplace drug testing.

What percentage of the average adult New Zealand population do you think has at least tried 'P' (methamphetamine) in the past 12 months? That's how she framed the revelation of her compelling information. People said 5, 10, 15, 40. It became like an auction. When she revealed the true answer – 15%, the room was deflated. The expectation had been skewed to 40%. (Remember anchoring and adjustment?) Even though a rational mind might still find 15% a disturbing answer, it wasn't enough to get signatures on order forms.

I had a chat with her over lunch as she had another presentation scheduled for the afternoon. I explained the power of misdirection and the reveal. She then added one slide to her PowerPoint show which showed the past five years' percentages: 0.15, 0.2, 0.6, 0.1, 1.2. She didn't ask people to guess a random number but people would have been guessing in their heads something like 1.8 or 2.2. When she suddenly revealed 15%, you could feel the gasp from the audience as well as hear it. She made three workplace drug testing sales directly afterwards and got a lot of warm leads. She achieved a significant gain with a minor communication adjustment, one based on a joke-writing technique. Zero cost with maximum benefits.

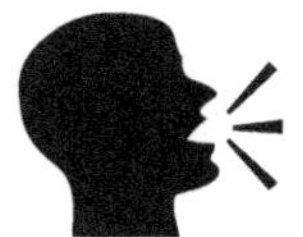

Make Change Irresistible

Do you know why the Americans have the disparaging term 'Limey' for the English? I don't mean, why do the Americans disparage the English? That's obvious. I mean, where did the term 'Limey' come from? In 1601, English Sailor John Lancaster discovered lime juice could cure scurvy. Despite being a cheap, easy and effective solution to a wide-spread problem, it took over 200 years to catch on. Change can be tough sometimes. The worth of an idea does not mean it gets adopted quicker.

Whether you're trying to lead a multi-million dollar corporate takeover or get the new guy to show up on time, you need to change people's behaviour. More accurately, you need to help people discover that they want or need to change. When it comes to change, the autonomy supportive leader needs to provide a personally meaningful reason to change.

Internal change must always precede external change. Ken Hultman in his book *Making Change Irresistible* wrote that people support change when they believe:

- Their needs are not currently being met.
- The change will make it easier for them to meet their needs.
- The benefits outweigh the costs/risks.
- The change will avoid a harm.
- The process is being handled properly.
- The process will work.
- The change is consistent with their values.
- Those responsible can be trusted.

People don't act on reality but on their perception of it. People's perceptions are viewed through the filters of their beliefs. Sociologist Morris Massey described the three phases of belief and values development in a young person's life.

Phase	
Imprinting	Absorbing and accepting, mainly from parents.
Modelling	Copying. Trying on values and beliefs like we try on clothes.
Socialisation	Largely influenced by peers and media. Searching for others like us.

A finding attributed to Massey that I found worrying was that, on average, 90% of people have their values determined by the age of ten. That's great, I suppose, if those are awesome values that will suit us as we grow and times and circumstances change. Personally, I'd prefer to choose my own values and beliefs, and help those I lead choose theirs wisely. What do we need to know before we go mucking about in the murky world of other people's beliefs and encouraging change?

There is risk in change. That's part of why many people are initially averse to it. But there is also risk in not changing. Identify that risk of not changing and draw it to their attention. There is a predictable process in people reacting to change as a form of loss, going through a cycle of denial, bargaining, anger, depression and acceptance. Be aware of where your people are at in the cycle as individuals react differently.

What looks like resistance is often a lack of clarity. 'Try harder,' is not useful commentary from a leader. 'Act healthier,' is not useful advice from a health ministry. But 'Buy low-fat milk,' might be.

In their book *Switch,* Dan and Chip Heath made popular the metaphor put forward by Jonathan Haidt in his book *The Happiness Hypothesis* of the elephant and the rider. Much of the psychology we've covered in this book revolves around the pros and cons of having a hugely powerful subconscious/automatic mind and a small but sensible conscious mind - the elephant and the rider. Neither is good or bad; both are essential but results are better if they work together. Goleman's emotional intelligence needs self awareness and self control; that's a skilled rider. If we leave our elephant in charge, it decides emotionally what we do and the rider changes job and becomes a lawyer, arguing our case after the damage is done.

Questions are a useful tool for leaders promoting or supporting change and dealing with resistance. Trying to be as non-threatening as possible, you can ask people to show you some proof. 'It'll never work,' provokes the question, 'What makes you say that?' Another useful question to get people asking questions and challenging imprinted beliefs themselves subconsciously (where it needs to happen) is, 'If the opposite were true, what proof is there of that?'

Participating in a community of believers strengthens our beliefs. Remember Solomon Asch and his line length experiments where 37% of people gave blatantly wrong answers simply because the group did? If you've got people with unhelpful beliefs together, that'll compound their unhelpful beliefs. Enlist people's social networks to support vital behaviours. If we stick with the elephant metaphor, we need to rally the herd. Break up groups that don't.

Remember the chapter on loss aversion? Interestingly, loss aversion doesn't just apply to tangible things we can possess in a physical sense. Our beliefs are possessions. People won't just give them away. Ridding someone of their anger or sadness doesn't make them happy – it makes them empty. However, it's more useful and people may accept *a swap* for equal or greater value. Here are some suggestions for replacement values for some unhelpful values your people might have.

Unhelpful Value	**Possible Replacement Value**
Preserving status quo	Developing one's potential
Being perfect	Improving on your best
Self interest	Mutual interest
Seeking recognition	Adding value
Expediency	Personal integrity
Self justification	Being honest with yourself
Posturing	Being genuine
Judging others	Accepting others

Every change situation requires its own strategy but they have commonalities. Hultman identifies eight characteristics of strategies for overcoming resistance:

1. Establish a positive climate (Losada's ratio).
2. Encourage an interest in improvement.
3. Show people how change can help them.
4. Help people increase their competence (Mastery).
5. Involve people in decisions (Autonomy).
6. Encourage people to value teamwork (Purpose).
7. Take emotions into account but try not to react emotionally yourself.
8. Concentrate on factors within your control (Realism).

Discuss the inevitable consequences of *not changing*.

Find emotional and experiential commonalities between differing individuals. In her book *Being Wrong*, author Kathryn Schultz describes the bitterest of conflicts in the 1960s in Durham, North Carolina. At a time where Government was imposing desegregation in schools, the Government agent in charge of the project needed two particularly conflicted individuals to work together. Ann Atwater was an African American mother and CP Ellis was a white KKK father. Despite their entrenched oppositions, and after much effort by the Government agent, he stumbled upon the emotional and experiential commonalities that eventually led them to working together successfully – they were both poor and they were both parents.

We attempt to understand new or complex things in relation to things we already know.

13.5% of the population are what marketers call 'Early Adopters' or 'Opinion Leaders'. This is as true for workplace changes as it is for buyers of the latest type of jeans. These are the people in your workplace you need onside early and often. Find and focus on them. Beware of 'Innovators'. They're different and the wrong kind of different at that. Innovators are visibly different, isolated and disrespect traditions. Early Adopters/Opinion Leaders are respected and connected. They're viewed as knowledgeable, trustworthy and are frequent interactors with others. The messenger is as important as the message.

The two core questions for individuals faced with a choice about changing behaviour are:

1. Is it worth it?
2. Can I do it?

These are the same two questions I posed in the first paragraph of this book, questions of motivation (is it worth it?) and ability (can I do it?) Answer these honestly, accurately and from the other's person's point of view and you'll go a long way to shifting them in favour of change.

How can you help someone with a poor track record in changing and achieving their goals? One method is 'self-priming' with 'when-then' statements about steps towards the goal. Let's say your goal is to keep the lawn mown. An example statement would be, '**WHEN** I see the lawnmower, **THEN** I will fill it with petrol **SO I CAN** mow the lawn.' The benefits of this approach are that it removes ambivalence, turns a negative into a positive, saves demand on our willpower tank and fosters a habit.

Nothing focuses the mind like surprise. The anterior cingulated cortex (ACC) kicks in when we make an erroneous prediction. You know when you're carrying the groceries down the steps and you take that last step which isn't there but you thought it was? Ding-ding goes the ACC. This is your brain telling to you to learn from this experience. It's right next to the Thalamus and the Hypothalamus. The Thalamus directs your conscious attention. The Hypothalamus directs physical actions such as the stress response.

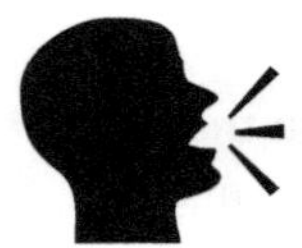

Putting It All Together

I've deliberately used a variety of examples in this book, from factories to offices to homes and people who don't ever work in the same place twice. People's brains follow much the same science, regardless of the nature or location of their work. I've heard arguments that so-called professionals are different – lawyers, doctors, accountants, engineers, etc. Leaders of these people can play a significant part in improving the motivational climate and in removing obstacles to individual motivation. They can demonstrate their own drive for results, provide appropriate recognition, encourage ideas and development, increase responsibility, get to know them individually and emphasise the interdependence of everyone's work.

Make sure your people feel like they are making progress. Much of what looks like laziness is simply avoidance. Remember not thinking about polar bears? Focus on what you want, not what you don't want.

Whether they're saying it out loud or not, the questions employees have are:

- What's important around here?
- How can I make a difference?
- What's in it for me if I do make a difference?

Most staff turnover occurs within the first eighteen months of employment yet recognition for length of service typically occurs at five or ten year milestones. Keep up the morning teas and novelty gifts for the lifers putting in their time if you wish to, but you'll be more effective as a leader if you put in some hard yards with those new people. They don't need a gold watch after three months but that's an ideal time in most roles for some face time with the boss. Hit them up with some questions and give them time to come up with considered responses:

- You've been here three months, how have we met and not met your expectations?
- What do you think we do best here?
- Is there anything you've seen done elsewhere that you think we could learn from?
- Have we done anything that might cause you to think about leaving?

We need to link personal goals to 'work well-being'. This is not the same as the overused term 'Work-Life Balance'. The diagram below on the left shows the recent notion of trying to juggle our work and non-work lives into some sort of predictable and even equilibrium. The reality for many already and more in future will be a changing and irregular overlap, as depicted in the diagram below on the right. I wish I could draw the Venn diagram with the circles moving and re-sizing because the pro-

Work-life balance

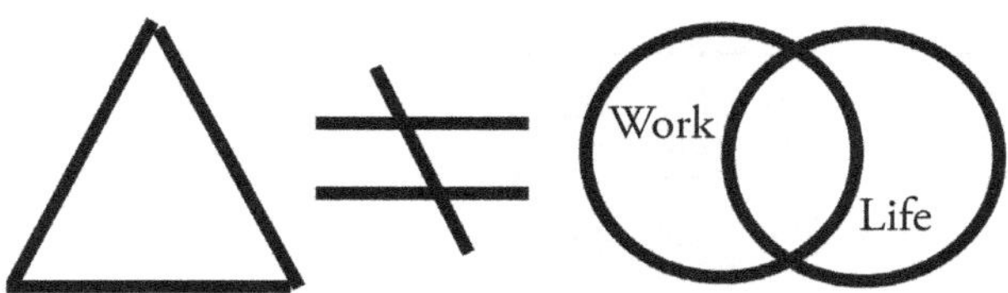

portions and relationships between our work and non-work lives fluctuate.

Thanks to those neurons and mirror neurons firing over and over again, they become more efficient. What was difficult becomes easier through practice, observation and feedback. This is why perseverance and 'grit' is so important for success. Leaders need to be on the look-out for frustration and/or lack of progress. They need to model 'grit' and limit distractions and interruptions. It doesn't have to be silence or violence. Make it safe to talk. Look for the mutuality. Create a common purpose. Tell stories to connect to feelings.

Reproduce the environment. If they're going to be scuba diving at work, then they need to learn the job underwater with tanks on their back and flippers on their feet.

Listen to what you think you mean to say versus the messages that actually get heard.

'I saw how you helped that customer.'	→	My boss notices what I do.
'What you just did is a perfect example of our company's value of x'	→	I am contributing to something bigger.
'This is one of your strengths.'	→	I can do better.
'I'd like to thank you for five years of service.'	→	I belong.

As Jim Collins and Jerry Porras say in their book *Built To Last*, resilient organisations espouse a *purpose* above and beyond simply making money. Create a feedback culture. Demonstrate a genuine interest. Recruit for values.

There's the popular view that sometimes owners start to look like their pets and remember Robert Zajonc's study on old married couples starting to look alike. My view is that workplaces tend to take on the personality of their leader and that this is what workplace culture is. Co-ownership of anything heightens engagement with it, shifting from the 'me' to the 'we'. Be less about *attracting* talent as you are about *matching* talent and *developing* talent.

JRA break engagement down into three types making up the whole: cognitive engagement (thinking), emotional engagement (feeling) and behavioural engagement (doing.) You can see behavioural engagement if you bother to look. You can't directly see the other two but there are clues to look for.

The problem often isn't that people aren't working hard enough, it's that they're working too hard. People avoid thinking by being too busy to think. A Brain-Based Boss knows this is short-term thinking and ultimately futile.

Psychiatrist Edward Hallowell in his book *Shine* identifies his five steps to creating an environment where leaders can bring out the best in their people. He says it's not rocket science: it's more complicated. It's *brain* science.

Looking at many modern workplaces, he saw a few repeated obstacles to a brain friendly environment:

- Social isolation and disconnection (the internet can both help and hinder this).
- Fear and insecurity.
- Information overload.
- Boundaryless and interruption-infested workplaces and practices.

Hallowell's five steps to shine are:

1. Select (the right people in the right jobs – what I would call 'fit').
2. Connect (strengthen interpersonal bonds in all directions).
3. Play (stimulating the hormone BDNF which triggers nerve growth in the brain).
4. Grapple and grow (enable people to overcome pressure through manageable challenges and move towards mastery. Sounds like 'Flow', eh).
5. Shine (stimulate loyalty and people's inherent desire to excel).

Leaders need to promote feelings of employees being challenged in their areas of skill, optimism and confidence. They need to prevent or mitigate feelings of being overwhelmed, cynicism, pessimism and fear. People need to feel stability. That doesn't mean never changing.

When you're in the planning stages of a project or change strategy, or even before that when you're budgeting, don't ask people how long they think it will take them to do it. Ask how long similar projects or tasks have taken others. It's a subtly different question but far more likely to generate realistic answers. Massive over-confidence riddles management planning based on many of the heuristics we're covered – over-optimism, planning around best-case scenarios rather than probable outcomes, etc.

The research of Kerry Patterson and his fellow authors of *Influencer* found that 88% of people working on major projects believe it will fail but plod along anyway. Only 10% felt it was OK to speak out. The phrase 'slow motion train wreck' was used.

One technique promoted by Guy Kawasaki is the 'project pre-mortem'. We all know post-mortems occur after the death of people (and projects). And they should for good reason – to learn why. The project pre-mortem is effectively exactly the same concept and process. The difference is in the timing and the usefulness. A post-mortem is useful for your next project (assuming anyone trusts you enough to ever assign you a project ever again). A pre-mortem is useful right now for the project you're about to initiate. During the initial planning stage, simply run some sessions with a cross-section of key people based on the assumption *that the project has already failed.* Start finding out why and work solutions into your planning while you still can.

Meaning matters; details don't. If you want to change how people behave, you first have to change *how* they think. Not *what* they think but *how* they think. There's a big difference. And the first person that needs to do so is you. There is no one right way. Before you can influence anything, you must specify what it is you're trying to influence. The key word here is *specify*.

Kerry Patterson et al propose a four-step process for influencing behaviour on large or small scales, based on a fundamental question for all leaders in any workplace. In order to improve our current situation, what must people actually do or stop doing?

1. Focus on behaviour.
2. Identify the vital few behaviours.
3. Identify recovery (replacement) behaviours.
4. Test and evaluate.

Positive deviance is a clue for leaders to look for. Look for high performing individuals in low performing groups. Dive into the centre of the department or community you want to change. Study the places where the problem should exist but doesn't. What are they doing or not doing differently? Identify the unique behaviours of the successful group or individual.

People choose their behaviours based on what they expect will happen to them afterwards. If we wish to alter behaviour, we need to alter people's mental maps of cause and effect. When it comes to resistant problems, verbal persuasion rarely works. If you ever do try to use verbal persuasion, the best method is stories. They are better recalled and have greater credibility with listeners. The great persuader is personal experience. As a leader with a person with such a resistant problem the best approach is to create a series of rapid, low-risk, mini-experiences with small increases in challenge. That's the same approach taken by oft-cited psychologist Albert Bandura in dealing with people with snake phobias.

'It ain't so much the things we don't know that get us into trouble. It's the things we do know that just ain't so.' – Artemus Ward

Over-confidence is one of the leading causes of human error. Doctors are successful, experienced, educated and qualified professionals and you'd want them to be confident, wouldn't you? How would you feel if you had a check-up and your doctor says, 'Phew. Wow. Um, I'll be back in five minutes, I really need to google this!'?

Chabris and Simons with their invisible gorilla and related studies looked at confidence too. They strongly connected incompetence with over-confidence. They say that the best doctors should display a range of confidence. Some doubt shows self awareness which is essential but others judge them on personality and appearances. Being confident in people we don't know is a signal of weakness. Variation in confidence in people we do know is a sign of strength.

But what price comes with that confidence? Atul Gawande writes of a study done in 2001 at John Hopkins Hospital by Peter Pronovost. I admit my working medical knowledge of medicine is from years of watching *E.R.* and *M.A.S.H.* (but never *Grey's Anatomy*). As a result, I know how to shout, 'Charge the paddles!' and, 'CLEAR!' really loudly but that's about it. I have heard them talking about 'putting in a central line'. It sounds common and important. It is.

A common and potentially fatal problem in the process of inserting a central line is infection, despite it being a common and important process that everyone learns and performs early and often. You'd expect a high degree of *confidence.* The study observed all the five-step central line insertions for a month. In more than third of patients, at least one step was skipped. By following and insisting on a simple checklist of the five critical steps, the doctors eventually reduced their infection rate over the first year from 11% to 0%. The checklist solved that infection problem but the real enemy wasn't bacteria – it was *over*-confidence.

Disconnection is one of the chief causes of poor performance in today's workplace but it is also one of the most easily fixed. Leaders need to promote positive connections of all kinds and identify and intervene on disconnections. Connection stabilises and propels people. Higher tech workplaces require even higher 'touch'. Ask anyone why they're happy and the answer, most likely, will involve a connection to a specific person. My own research shows that most of the main negative reasons people leave a workplace are due to disconnection from their immediate supervisor or a colleague they cannot avoid. A poll by Gallup Management journal showed that when people leave their job, 70% of the time, they're not leaving their job, they're leaving their manager.

Sarah Burgard from the University of Michigan has shown that job insecurity (fear) causes more illness than actually losing a job. Disconnected employees are more likely to get sick and more likely to miss work. A study by the Confederation of British Industry estimated that 15% of illness days taken were not due to actual illnesses. In 2007, Gallup research found that 'having a best friend at work' increased the likelihood of someone being engaged at work by 700%. Connection lessens fear. Some fears are valid – otherwise it's just denial – but fear inhibits productivity and makes people play 'not to lose' rather than to win.

Here's one last story to make a point. If you like, the point could be about the risks in encouraging people to play 'not to lose' rather than to win. It's a great story and a true one – the two often don't go together. It can make a number of other points but you can think about those as and after you read it.

Maybe where you're from you went along as a kid or parent in the summer to baseball or softball games. We went along to cricket. On a warm summer's morning, you sit with other parents with the smell of freshly cut grass in your nostrils, the warmth of the sunshine on your skin. Maybe you're sitting in a discount foldout chair and trying to avoid eye contact as the parents debate whose turn it is to go and get coffees for everyone.

You don't need to know the technicalities of cricket to roll along with this story. You get the scene, the participants and the context.

My son was quite the cricketer growing up. This particular game was the grand final of the season and, as in all such stories, they were playing their arch enemy in the final – their mortal nemesis. Twice they had met in the regular season and each team had won once by the narrowest of margins. Fittingly they met again in the last game of the season upon which their success would be judged and remembered.

My son's team batted first and did quite well. The other team batting second also did quite well. With only two balls left to be bowled in the game, they needed six runs to win – challenging but do-able.

The bowler delivered the penultimate delivery. The opposition batsman hit it well but directly to my son. The batsman was confident so he set off for the run but then noticed that my son had the ball in hand. Caught in no-man's land, time seemed to stand still as the batsman hesitated to continue then turned to make his way back. By this time, my son had hurled the ball at the stumps.

He had fielded the ball directly side-on to the stumps – the three sticks in the ground that the ball needed to hit to get the batsman out. Front-on, it would have been a challenging throw but side-on, it was almost impossible with only one stump to aim at. My son hurled it as the batsman scampered back and ...

... the ball missed the stumps, missed all the other fielders and went all the way across the field for four overthrow runs. They had needed six runs to win. Now they only needed two runs to win with the last ball still to be bowled.

Since it was a kids' grade, the coaches were also the umpires and the umpire standing out next to my son happened to be the coach of my son's team. He took this moment, what he saw as a 'teachable moment', to step across and suggest, in a loving and nurturing way, that if those exact same set of circumstances should ever occur again, then the sensible thing to do would be to let the batsman take a single run and walk the ball in closer to the stumps to prevent them taking a second run rather than risking overthrows for the sake of an unlikely out. 'Do you understand?' he asked as he sought confirmation. My son confirmed it.

Last ball. Two runs to win. One run to tie.

So, the same bowler came in to bowl the last ball of the last game of the season. He bowled the same type of delivery to the same batsman who played the same type of shot to the same place on the field where my son picked it up and...

... without a moment's hesitation hurled it at the stumps, knocking them out of the ground and, winning the game, being carried off the ground on the shoulders of his team-mates.

I remember it vividly, not just because of the dramatic win, but because our coach remained standing where he was, his head in his hands which he slowly shook disbelievingly as the unlikely chaos ensued around him.

Next time, like my son's coach, you think you're in a teachable moment with someone you're trying to lead or convince yourself you're motivating them, remember that the environment motivates them more than you ever could, limited by the extent of their own self awareness, and driven by their internal needs for Mastery, Autonomy and Purpose.

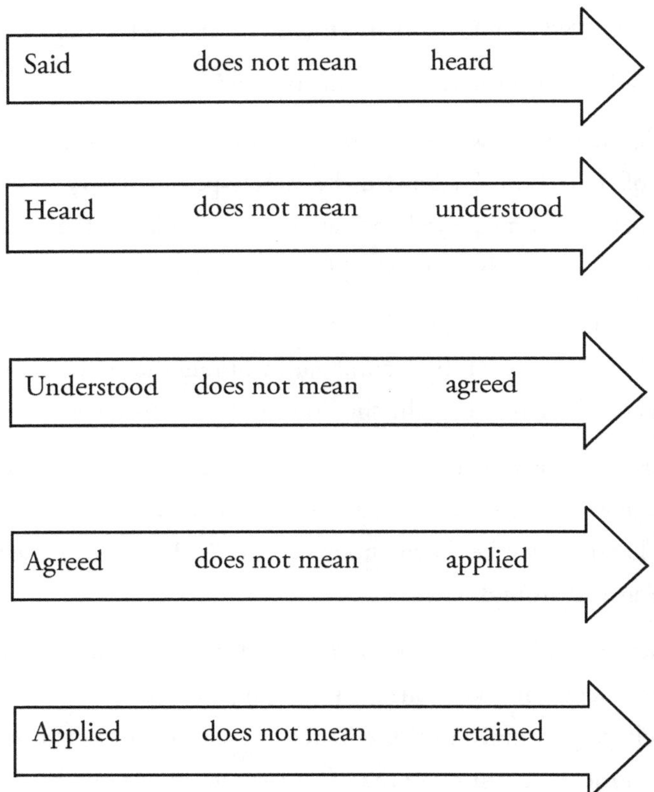
Said does not mean heard
Heard does not mean understood
Understood does not mean agreed
Agreed does not mean applied
Applied does not mean retained

Section 4

Brain-Based Boss Employee Checklist: Looking For Clues

- How congruent are they? (Are their words reinforced by their voice and actions?)
- To what extent do they ever think about how they think?
- What evidence is there of their engagement level – making discretionary effort?
- How aligned are their personal values with the values they need at work?
- Are they a 'deferrer' or a 'grabber'?
- How's their 'grit' level – How quick are they to seek out help?
- Have they got a 'fixed' or a 'growth' mindset? ('I am' vs 'I do').
- Are their optimism levels appropriate? Listen for universals like 'always' or 'never'. How do they react to setbacks?

- How do they make decisions? To what extent do they need or choose to involve others?
- How 'calibrated' are they between their real and their self-perceived abilities?
- When and how do they seek feedback to improve their performance?
- How aware are they of their performance gaps?
- 'Flow' – How comfortable are they in challenging situations? What proportion of their time is spent in high skill and high challenge activities? How often are they distracted or interrupted?
- Do they speak in the voice of 'Self 1?' ('Don't do this or that.')
- To what extent do they take responsibility for their own learning?
- What is the ratio of positive to negative comments? (Looking for >3:1)
- Do they question the reasons why 'things are done the way they are around here?'
- 'Inattentional Blindness' – Do they notice small or subtle changes?

- To what extent are they OK with 'rough enough is good enough'?
- How do they solve problems?
- Are they over-influenced by first impressions?
- How concerned are they by others' opinions of them?
- How often do they help others out, generating the potential for reciprocity?
- What's their reaction to formal authority?
- How have they organised their own personal workspace?
- To what extent and in what way do they refer to their future self?
- To what extent and in what way do they recognise the efforts of others?
- When changes are proposed, how do they describe their expectations?
- How do they react to the prospect of even minor risk?
- To what extent do they compare themselves to others? What others?

- How do others respond to requests they make?
- When explaining to others or making requests of them, how do they use framing to set expectations?
- To what extent, and how, do they track their own progress?
- When and how do they deal with conflict?

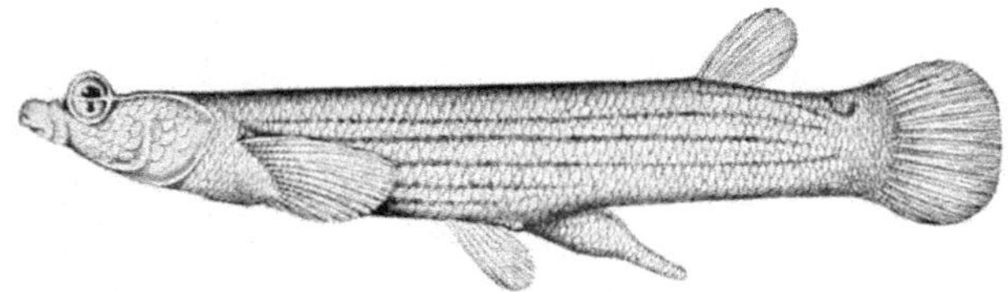

Bibliography

Dan Ariely *Predictably Irrational* (Harper Collins, 2009)

Angela Atkins *Management Bites* (Harper Collins, 2009)

John Baldoni *Great motivation secrets of great leaders* (McGraw Hill, 2005)

Iris Barrow *How to lead and motivate others* (Reed, 1995)

Gene Bedell *3 steps to yes: The gentle art of getting your way* (Crown Business, 2000)

Ori Brafman and Rom Brafman *Sway: The irresistable pull of irrational behaviour* (Virgin Books, 2009)

Ori Brafman and Rom Brafman *Click: The magic if instant connections* (Broadway Books, 2010)

Leigh Branham *The 7 hidden reasons employees leave* (Amacom, 2005)

Dan Buettner *The Blue Zone* (National Geographic, 2008)

Christopher Chabris and Daniel Simons *The invisible gorilla* (Harper Collins, 2010)

Robert L Cialdini *Yes: 50 scientifically proven ways to be persuasive* (Free Press, 2009)

Robert L Cialdini *Influence: The psychology of persuasion* (Collins Business Essentials, 2006)

Mihaly Csikszentmihalyi *Flow: The psychology of optimal experience* (Harper Collins, 1990)

Mihaly Csikszentmihalyi *Good business: Leadership, flow and the making of meaning* (Viking 2003)

Janet Davison and Robert Sternberg *The psychology of problem solving* (Cambridge University Press, 2003)

Edward L Deci *Why we do what we do: Understanding self motivation* (Penguin Books, 1995)

Carol S Dweck *Mindset: The new psychology of success* (Random House, 2006)

David Eaglemen *Incognito: The secret lives of the brain* (Canongate Books, 2011)

Linda Edgecombe *Boost: Engaging and energizing teams* (Insomniac Press, 2010)

Alan Fairweather *How to be a motivational manager* (How to books, 2007)

Patrick Forsyth *How to motivate people* (Kogan Page, 2006)

W Timothy Gallway *The inner game of work* (Random House, 2001)

Howard Gardner *Changing minds* (Harvard Business School Press, 2004)

Atul Gawande *The Checklist Manifesto* (Profile Books, 2009)

Thomas Gilovich *How we know what isn't so* (The Free Press, 1991)

Adrian Gostick Chester Elton *The carrot principle* (Simon & Schuster, 2009)

Adrian Gostick Chester Elton *A carrot a day* (Gibbs Smith, 2004)

Adrian Gostick Chester Elton *The orange revolution* (The Free Press, 2010)

Russell Granger *The 7 triggers to yes* (McGraw Hill, 2008)

Jonathan Haidt *The happiness hypothesis* (William Heinemann, 2006)

Joseph T Hallinan *Errornomics: Why we make mistakes* (Broadway Books, 2009)

Edward M Hallowell *Shine: Using brain science to get the best from your people* (Harvard Business Review Press, 2011)

Chip Heath and Dan Heath *Made to stick: Why Some Ideas Survive and Others Die* (Random House, 2007)

Chip Heath and Dan Heath *Switch: How to change things when change is hard* (Crown Business, 2010)

Ken Hultman *Making change irresistible* (Davies-Black Publishing, 1998)

Ross Jay *Build a great team* (Prentice Hall, 1995)

Daniel Kahneman *Thinking, fast and slow* (Allen Lane, 2011)

Guy Kawasaki *Enchantment: The art of changing hearts, minds and actions* (Portfolio / Penguin, 2011)

Daniel Kehoe *Motivating employees* (McGraw Hill, 2007)

Alfie Kohn *Punished By Rewards* (Houghton Mifflin Harcourt, 1993)

Kathy Kolbe *Powered by instinct: 5 rules for trusting your guts* (Momentus Press, 2004)

Jonah Lehrer *How we decide* (Houghton Mifflin Harcourt, 2009)

Frank Luntz *Words that work* (Hyperion, 2007)

David Macleod and Chris Brady *The extra mile* (Prentice Hall, 2008)

Kelly McGonigal *The Willpower Instinct* (Penguin, 2012)

David McRaney *You Are Not So Smart* (Gotham Books, 2011)

Corrine Maier *Hello laziness: Why hard work doesn't pay* (Orion, 2004)

John Medina *Brain rules* (Pear Press, 2008)

Caroline Miller and Michael Frisch *Creating your best life* (Sterling, 2009)

Bob Nelson and Dean Spitzer *The 1001 rewards and recognition fieldbook* (Workman Publishing, 2003)

Jay Niblick *What's your genius?* (St James Books, 2009)

Aryanne Oade *Building influence in the workplace* (Palgrave Macmillan, 2010)

Kerry Patterson and Joseph Grenny *Influencer: The Power to change anything* (McGraw Hill, 2008)

Kerry Patterson and Joseph Grenner *Crucial conversations* (McGraw Hill, 2002)

Daniel H Pink *Drive: The surprising truth about what motivates us* (Canongate Books, 2010)

Richard Restak *Think smart* (Riverhead Books, 2009)

John Robertson *Road to success* (JRA Associates, 2011)

Kathryn Schultz *Being wrong* (Harper Collins, 2010)

Dov Seidman *How* (John Wiley & Sons, 2007)

Martin E.P. Seligman *What you can change and what you can't* (First Vintage Books, 1993)

Martin E.P. Seligman *Learned Optimism* (First Vintage Books, 2006)

Martin E.P. Seligman *Flourish* (Simon & Schuster, 2011)

Daniel J Siegel *Mindsight: The new science of personal transformation* (Bantam Books, 2010)

Geoff Smith *Leading the professionals* (Kogan Page, 2004)

James Surowiecki *The Wisdom Of Crowds* (Anchor Books, 2004)

Richard Thaler and Cass Sunstein *Nudge* (Penguin Books, 2008)

Kaye Thorne *Managing the mavericks* (Chandos Publishing, 2001)

Richard Wiseman *59 seconds* (MacMillan, 2009)

Rob Yeung *I is for influence* (MacMillan, 2011)